THE BOOK OF
PERSONALITY
TESTS

25 Easy to Score Tests
that Reveal the Real You

Haulwen Nicholas

WELLFLEET

P R E S S

Brimming with creative inspiration, how-to projects, and useful information to enrich your everyday life, Quarto Knows is a favorite destination for those pursuing their interests and passions. Visit our site and dig deeper with our books into your area of interest: Quarto Creates, Quarto Cooks, Quarto Homes, Quarto Lives, Quarto Drives, Quarto Explores, Quarto Gifts, or Quarto Kids.

Inspiring | Educating | Creating | Entertaining

This edition published in 2020
by Wellfleet Press,
an imprint of The Quarto Group,
142 West 36th Street, 4th Floor,
New York, NY 10018, USA
T (212) 779-4972 F (212) 779-6058
www.QuartoKnows.com

Wellfleet titles are also available at discount for retail, wholesale, promotional, and bulk purchase. For details, contact the Special Sales Manager by email at specialsales@quarto.com or by mail at The Quarto Group, Attn: Special Sales Manager, 100 Cummings Center Suite 265D, Beverly, MA 01915 USA.

10 9 8 7 6 5 4 3 2

Library of Congress Control Number: 2020938545

ISBN: 978-0-7858-3860-9

Senior Commissioning Editor: Eszter Karpati
Editor: Gillian Haslam
Deputy Art Director: Martina Calvio
Designer: Josse Pickard
Publisher: Samantha Warrington

Printed in Singapore

MIX
Paper from
responsible sources
FSC™ C007207

CONTENTS

MEET HAULWEN

As I was writing this book, I read a prompt on social media about my Myers Briggs® personality type and how that type communicates. As I read it, I had one of those light-bulb moments, saying "ahh, so I'm not the only one." I forwarded it to my husband and he agreed: "yes, you tick every one of those," and as usual he was amused at my need for this validation. Seeing the comments of other people with the same "type" as me, saying they did the same, gave me a sense of belonging and that perhaps I'm not quite as odd as I think I am. It wasn't telling me something I didn't already know about myself, but it was confirming to me that I'm not the only one who does it and it made me realize, yet again, that it's OK to be like this. I don't have to hide who I am to "fit in" with societal norms and that for me is the joy of personality types, it's not telling you that you are someone different to who you think you are. It's confirming to you "who you are," so that you can accept yourself, especially in a world where there are more and more expectations to be something that you aren't.

Writing this book has brought together my passion and interest in personality types that I've had since I was at school, doing the tests in my childhood annuals which ranged from what sort of psychic I was, to what personality I was due to my eye color. I always have felt like the oddball, looking in at a world I struggled to interact with, and although I've never really wanted to fit in, it is nice to connect with others and feel a sense of belonging. Personality type testing has helped me to understand myself and reconnect with who I am, and has helped me to bring balance and deal with stress, exhaustion, anxiety, and long-term health issues.

What I discovered from personality type testing was that I was continually operating outside my natural preferences. I wasn't spending time recharging in the best way for me, and eventually I burnt out and was diagnosed with Chronic Fatigue Syndrome/M.E.

Since I've reconnected with who I am, my life has turned around. I know what exhausts me, I know what I prefer to do when, and with it I feel more alive than I can remember. It didn't teach me anything I didn't already know, it just reminded me of it and sometimes in a world where we wear a hundred masks, we just need to step back and drop them for a while, to recharge and be ourselves. I now take pleasure in helping others reconnect with who they are through my coaching in SMEs or with individuals on a one-to-one basis or via my online coaching.

I will forever be fascinated by personality tests and love to read about new ones, whether fun ones on the internet or new developmental techniques for organizations. I also know that some of these tests are quite daunting and when you first get your results it's really hard to know what to do with this information, which is why I hope this fun book will make it an easy introduction and if you want to know more, just pop to the back for some further resources and reading.

Every day I am reminded again of what I love and every day I am reminded of what my personality strengths and development opportunities are. Personality type testing will be something I use to help me grow and develop throughout my life. It will continue to remind me of my preferences, to remind me how to recharge, and to remind me where I can go to develop myself and grow my comfort zone. That's why I really hope you'll enjoy this book. It gives you an introduction to these tests, but in a relaxed way which I've made easy to understand. Why not use these tests as an ice breaker, or use them with family and friends? Have some fun and, who knows, along the way you might discover something about you that you knew but had never really acknowledged.

INTRODUCTION

Personality type tests—you either love them or you hate them, but even if you're in the latter camp, you're probably still intrigued by them and perhaps do the odd one without telling anyone, and that's why you're reading this book, isn't it?

What is it about personality type testing that we find so fascinating? Social media and magazines are full of fun tests that you can share with your family and friends. So why do you do them? Why do you want to know what color you are? Are you an empath? What Hogwarts house you are in? Where is your ideal place to live? What type of spirit animal are you? Are you a leader or a follower?

A lot of the time you take the light-hearted tests in magazines and on social media to have a bit of a laugh, though deep down there may be other things you are searching for:

Validation—Some of you will want to validate your behaviors or to validate the way you think and feel. Seeing words on paper stating that this "type" behaves in this way or that way can make you feel "normal," and this can help you to express yourself more honestly (or dishonestly), depending on who you are.

Self-discovery—For others it may be a sense of wanting to discover something new about yourself, though to be honest most of you will do a test and it will remind you of your traits rather than telling you something you don't already know. So, it's a journey of re-discovery rather than self-discovery. Sometimes you can forget your own strengths and your own weaknesses, and having a test remind you of this can help you to look at opportunities for learning and growth.

Finding our tribe—As humans we naturally long to find a place to belong, yet as more and more people work globally, at home alone, away from our local communities with little interaction with others, life can feel lonely. These tests can help you to find your tribe and give you a sense of belonging in a world where perhaps you don't feel like you fit in. Or it could just be about wanting to belong to a "gang" of like-minded individuals where you can band together and feel "safe."

Understanding others—It may be that you long to relate to the people around you, to understand their point of view, and to learn how to interact better with them. Though a minority of people will want to use it to try to manipulate others, most just want to be able to put themselves in the shoes of the people around them, to show they have empathy for their situation.

Categorization—For some people, life is easier when you can categorize people, then in your mind you can make "assumptions" on a person because of their type and "deal" with them accordingly. However, no one is ever really 100% their "type" all the time, so this can be flawed.

Increasingly, more and more organizations are using personality type testing, and this may be where you do your first in-depth personality type test. It can help managers to build teams, deal with conflict, improve communications, and in some organizations these tests are also used in the interview process. Of course, the thing to remember is that these tests are only a snapshot in time and if you answer how you think you should answer, rather than answering honestly and openly, then it won't help you or the organization. But when used in the correct way, they are a good tool for helping individuals and companies to learn and grow.

Whatever the reasons you do these tests, most of you will use them as a fun and friendly way to get to know friends and family and understand yourself, and that is the purpose of this book. Enjoy.

HISTORY AND CONTEXT

When we think about personality type testing, it can be easy to think of it as a way to "put people in a box" and often in human society we like to do that, whether it is identifying people by their social status, their intellect, their job title, or by what type of car they drive. It can sometimes seem easier to assume that all people who tick these boxes behave in this way, rather than accept each person as an individual.

This is where we have to put personality type tests into context. They are a preference, just as while we have a preference for being left-handed or right-handed, we are still able to write with the other hand if we injure the hand we prefer to write with. Over time, if we still had to use our non-preferred hand, we would learn to write as well with this one as our preferred one. Personality traits are the same. We have certain traits we are more familiar with and these are our preferences, but over time we can "learn" how to use the other preferences so we become more balanced—this means we can grow, change, and develop, but fundamentally we still have a preference that feels most comfortable to us. There are, of course, some instances where these preferences become a personality disorder as the preferences that a person is using are not acceptable in normal society, but for the most part the personality preferences we exhibit are just that and, if we are willing, we can develop these preferences and acquire new skills when we want to.

Over the last century there have been countless studies into the human mind, and this research continues to evolve, but personality type testing is still something people find fascinating. In fact, we first saw evidence of this with the Ancient Greeks where Hippocrates developed a theory known as the four humors, which is still referenced by some today.

Basically, his theory stated that the human body is made up of four substances. The theory refers to these substances as "humors." For ideal health, they have to be in perfect balance. When this balance is lost, it leads to sickness. These humors (and their associated moods) are Sanguine (optimist), Choleric (irritable), Melancholic (depressed), and Phlegmatic (calm). Shakespeare used these humors to help develop his characters for his plays.

Other common forms of personality profiling are linked to astrological symbols and spirit animals. Both of these are ancient traditions, but when you view them through modern eyes you can see they were a means of characterizing human behaviors. Of course, since then, there has been a lot of investigation into the human persona so let's start by understanding what we mean by personality.

What is personality?

"Personality" is a term that refers to different parts of a person's character. It usually deals with virtually all human behavior, including mental, emotional, social, physical, and spiritual, although there are suggestions that there are aspects of an individual that aren't visible and we don't understand.

As humans we are complex creatures, but we long to bring order to everything around us, including defining people. Psychologists are constantly looking to define and categorize people. Understanding why people behave in different ways and why we are all unique are questions that still encourage lots of research. In particular, there is a lot of study into those with pathological tendencies compared to those without. Where would we be without all our crime thrillers looking at the psychological behavior of the criminal mind?

Psychologists continually look to predict behaviors amongst people so that they can predict future outcomes. This can help in all sorts of areas such as the workplace, sport, dealing with crisis and post-traumatic stress, parenting, and education, to name but a few. By understanding the personality of people, psychologists hope to be able to control and change the environment to bring about change.

There are several theories out there that try to define this, but there are two men who were seen as being at the forefront in understanding human personality—Sigmund Freud and Carl Jung.

Sigmund Freud

Sigmund Freud (1856-1939) was an Austrian neurologist and the founder of psychoanalysis. According to his theory, the single layer of the unconscious mind is divided into three parts. That is the id, ego, and superego.

- The id is usually present at birth. This represents the instinctive drives that a person has.
- The ego begins to develop at birth. This component controls the id in order to adapt to the changes that are taking place outside in the world. It brings a balance between the superego and id in the course of life.
- The superego is a component that begins to develop about 6 years of age. It's the component which controls the id. It's usually associated with the moral values and the conscience.

There is a lot more to his theory than can be described here, but basically, he determined that events that happen within our environment can cause conflict between these three parts of the mind—the id, ego, and superego. This conflict is usually a direct result of behavior in response to the world around us. At times these conflicts lead to changes in personality, as a person develops and learns to cope with these events.

Freud theorized that there were then five stages of personality development—from birth to one, from one to three years, from three to six years, six to adolescence, and adolescence. At each of these stages in life the child's personality is developed, which results in adult behaviors and overall personality. Any challenges in each of those stages could have a positive or negative impact on personality development.

This is overly simplistic but hopefully it gives you a very basic idea of his theories.

Carl Jung

Carl Jung (1875-1961) was a Swiss psychologist and psychiatrist and the founder of Analytical Psychology.

Like Freud, he had similar thoughts about the unconscious mind and personality. However, he had a different approach as he proposed that the unconscious consists of two layers, rather than one.

Jung called the first layer the Personal Unconscious, and basically it's the same as Freud's version of the unconscious as described above. That is, it houses material from a person's life that is within their conscious awareness because it has been repressed or forgotten. This is directly next to the ego and it is completely below conscious awareness.

The second layer, Jung proposed, was something deeper, which he called the Collective Unconscious. In basic terms, the collective unconscious is a store of traces of memory inherited from our ancestral past that is shared with the entire human race. Jung named these ancestral memories "archetypes," which then influence personality. They are not memories of actual personal experiences.

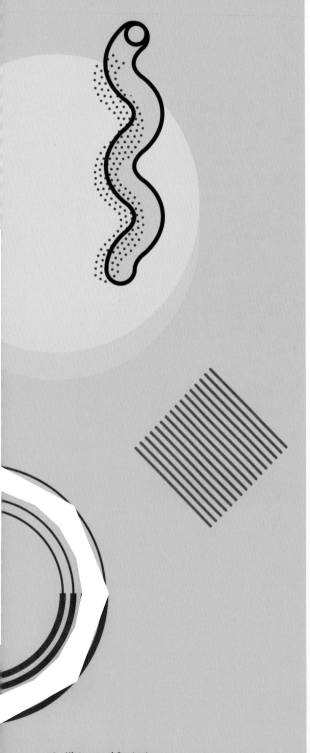

Instead, archetypes are emotionally charged images and thoughts that have universal meaning. These archetypal images and ideas show up frequently in dreams and are often manifested in culture's use of symbols in art, literature, and religion. According to Jung, a person's mind contains an unconscious part which is shared by all people. This region is usually developed over time and it is usually transferred from one generation to another.

How does this relate to personality tests?

Well, think about how we react to certain images dependent on our societal expectations, such as the mother as a nurturer. It means that due to cultural, local, and societal expectations, we respond to this, and other, external images in a certain way. These "archetype" symbols have a special status attached to them, gained across generations and the significant role they play in day-to-day life. As we adopt the local roles and norms that go with living with other people, these impact our personality development. I'm sure you can think of many symbols and roles that impact how you react in the world.

Jung went on to theorize more aspects of the personality, including:

- The animus and anima, which bring out the aspect of being male or feminine.
- The shadow, which represents the dark and the more primitive side of the personality.
- The self, which is what makes the person unite all of the other aspects to bring out their individual nature.

Jung also observed that human behavior tends to follow certain basic patterns, which become the natural preference of the person (like being left- or right-handed, as mentioned earlier). The preferred behavior gradually becomes a habit and leads to predictable personality traits. He described these as:

- Introversion, where the energy is turned to the internal world, or
- Extroversion, where the energy is turned to the outer world.

From this, he went on to develop four different functions:

- Thinking—People with this preference tend to have logical and questioning minds.
- Feeling—People with this preference tend to make judgments about how they value things, i.e. whether something is agreeable or not.
- Sensation—People with this preference tend to rely on sensory impressions. They review the world on how things look, what words sound like, and so on.
- Intuition—People with this preference tend to be aware of possibilities, looking at the wider implications which might not be known consciously through normal senses.

Each person would have a preference toward one of these functions, which then determines how they react to an experience. Upbringing and social conditions would lead to an individual placing a different emphasis on each of these four functions and when combined with the main psychic attitudes of extroversion and introversion, this would lead to eight different psychological types:

- Extrovert thinking—This type is led by rational thinking and logic. They tend to think their view of the world is the correct one and love order and facts.
- Introvert thinking—This type is more interested in the inner world of ideas rather than looking at the external world of facts. They are constantly questioning and formulating theories about things.
- Extrovert feeling—This type tends to be quite conventional and concerned with personal success. They handle people well and fit well into their peer group.
- Introvert feeling—This type can seem remote and inward looking. They enjoy peace and quiet and can come across as reserved.
- Extrovert sensation—This type is interested in the objects and sensations in the outside world. They tend to accept the world as it is and enjoy life.
- Introvert sensation—This type tends to focus on experienced sensation and can appear out of touch with the real world, finding it hard to express themselves.
- Extrovert intuitive—This type tends to get bored easily and likes to explore new ideas. They rely on their intuition to make decisions or judgments.
- Introvert intuitive—This type tends to focus on the mystical world of dreams, visions, and their collective unconscious. They are often preoccupied with inner daydreams and fantasies.

When we look at the many personality type tests that have been developed, we can really see how they relate to the work of Freud, but in particular that of Jung. However, Jung himself argued that it was rare for someone to conform to a single type and that matters were always complicated by people having other functions (auxiliary functions) and shadow personalities, which aren't always that obvious. He insisted that all humans are fluid dynamic beings and the types were preferences that were developed throughout their lives.

The "big five"

Since then, many great psychologists have gone on to develop these theories, although there are too many to go into detail here. One that has also greatly influenced modern personality type testing is The Five Factor Model of Personality, also known as the "big five" personality traits.

This began with the research of D.W. Fiske in 1949 and has been analyzed and developed over many years by many researchers, including Ernest Tupes and Raymond Christal in 1961, J.M. Digman in 1990, and further developed by Lewis Goldberg, Paul Costa Jr., and Robert R. McCrae, to name but a few of those who have investigated this over the decades.

These "big five" are wide-ranging categories of personality traits and although there is a lot of literature supporting this five-factor model of personality, researchers don't always agree on the exact labels for each of them.

Each of the five personality factors represents a range between two extremes. For example, extraversion represents a continuum between extreme extraversion and extreme introversion. In reality, most people lie somewhere in between the two opposite ends of each dimension. These five categories are usually described as follows and either use the Acronym OCEAN or CANOE as indicated below.

OCEAN (openness, conscientiousness, extraversion, agreeableness, and neuroticism)

CANOE (conscientiousness, agreeableness, neuroticism, openness, and extraversion)

Openness—Imagination and insight. People who are high in this trait tend to have a wide range of interests. They are curious about the world, love to learn new things, and enjoy new experiences.

Conscientiousness—Thoughtfulness, good impulse control, and goal-directed behaviors. People who are high in this trait tend to be organized and mindful of details.

Extraversion (or extroversion)—Excitable, sociable, talkative, assertive, with high amounts of emotional expression. People who are high in this trait are outgoing and tend to gain energy in social settings. Being with other people makes them feel energized and excited.

Agreeableness—Trust, altruism, kindness, affection. People who are high in this trait tend to be more cooperative and empathic.

Neuroticism—Sadness, moodiness, and emotional instability. People who are high in this trait tend to experience mood swings, anxiety, irritability, and sadness. Those low in this trait tend to be more stable and emotionally resilient.

It is now widely believed that these five personality traits are universal and can be used across a wide variety of cultures. Studies also suggest these traits have biological origins and are part of the human evolutionary process, and research continues in this area of psychology.

In conclusion, both Sigmund Freud and Carl Jung had a similar perspective regarding human personality. In this sense, they embraced the fact that the unconscious mind played a major role in personality development. However, their backgrounds influenced their differing views to a great extent. Furthermore, it is worth noting that the differences which ensued from their practice and theory have contributed a great deal to the field of psychology. This has gone on to influence things such as the "big five" personality traits and other such theories, some of which we cover in the next section of this book. This includes NLP communication model, Myers Briggs®, and Insights® to name but a few of the most well-known theories.

HOW TO DO THE TESTS

For each test over the coming pages, read through the introduction and then look at the questions. Remember that there are no wrong or right answers. Don't think too much about the questions, choose the answer that resonates with you. Make a note of your answers in the book or on a piece of paper, then go to the answers page to add up your score and find out your result. For all tests except for number 5, which details how to make your choices within the test, you will find two ways to do the test:

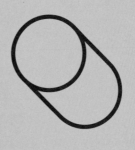

· Numerical: when you look at the answers, you will find a number next to the letter you have circled as your answer to the question. Add up all these numbers for your result.
· Symbol: when you look at the answers, you will find a symbol next to the letter you have circled as your answer to the question. Keep count of each symbol to find out your result.

What happens if your results are equal for two or more personality preferences? Why do you get different answers when you do the test multiple times? Don't worry. When these outcomes happen, there are a number of things to consider:

· Read through the preferences and see which one feels most like you. Only you truly know who you are, and these tests are a reminder.
· When and where you did the test? Were you relaxed? Did you answer honestly? If you aren't sure, take a break and do the test another time.

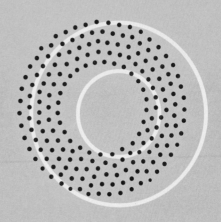

If you want to know more, check out the resources section on page 142.

1

ARE YOU AN INTROVERT OR AN EXTROVERT?

Being an introvert or an extrovert isn't an indication of how loud or quiet you are, but rather an indication of where your preference is for gaining energy. Knowing this can really help you to recognize where you draw your energy from and what to avoid to stop you feeling so tired. This knowledge can help you in all aspects of your life and allow you to make decisions on how to preserve your energy in the right way for you.

Myers-Briggs Type Indicator (MBTI)®

This test has been inspired by Myers-Briggs® Indicator. The Myers-Briggs® assessment is based on the theories of psychologist Carl Jung, but was further developed by the mother-and-daughter team of Katharine Briggs and Isabel Briggs Myers.

They developed a system that describes eight personality preferences and 16 personality type combinations. They wanted to translate Jung's ideas into an easy-to-understand framework, emphasizing that there are no better or worse personality types. For Isabel Myers, the development of the Myers-Briggs® questionnaire and the subsequent research and refinement of the instrument became her life's work. Her mission was to allow people to constructively use their difference to become empowered to make better decisions about their lives. The four dimensions of type that the mother-and-daughter team produced are:

1. Extraversion or introversion: your preference for where you get or focus your energy.
2. Sensing or intuition: your preference for the kind of information you gather and trust.
3. Thinking or feeling: your preference for making decisions.
4. Judging or perceiving: your preference for interacting with the world around you.

Please go to the resources section (page 142) to find out more on Myers-Briggs®.

Question 1

At the end of a busy day, what exercise do you prefer to do?

a. A gentle walk alone in nature.
b. Straight to the gym for a high intensity workout class.
c. Head to the gym, but prefer to wear headphones and then chat with people you know when you feel like it.

Question 2

How do you prefer to celebrate a special occasion?

a. With a select group of friends or family for a meal.
b. A meal at home on your own or with your partner or close friend.
c. A big party with everyone you know.

Question 3

You've been asked to attend a large conference/event—how do you feel?

a. Excited, you love the buzz and the interaction with new people.
b. It would depend on the event, but as long as you get some quiet time at some point it will probably be fun.
c. It fills you with dread and you secretly hope that something will happen to prevent you from attending.

Question 4

At a party, where will we find you?

a. In the kitchen or other quiet area helping out.
b. In the midst of it all, socializing with everyone.
c. On the dance floor (you can't make small talk on the dance floor), with retreats to the bathroom every so often for some quiet time.

Question 5

You are in a meeting where you are being taken through a detailed presentation on a new process. Everyone has been asked to be quiet and to discuss at the end of the meeting. What do you think?

a. Frustrated, as you like to talk things through in the meeting and you lose energy in these environments where there is little interaction.
b. It depends on the topic and what the person presenting is like, but it could be useful to just listen without feeling the need to interject.
c. It gives you time to reflect and listen so you can pull together your questions, which you will ask when they get to you in the conversation.

Question 6

You have just been informed that rather than being sat in individual offices, you are all going to move to an open-plan space shared with two other departments. How do you react?

a. Panic—you find background noise and a stimulating environment really distracting. You need space to concentrate, quiet time to think things through, and prefer a calm environment.
b. As long as there are some quiet break-out rooms where you can go when you need it, then it will be fine. Sometimes it's good to have a bit of noise around.
c. Overjoyed—you hate working on your own and like to interact with others. You love the buzz of a busy environment and prefer to have some noise in the background.

Question 7

You are feeling stressed and overwhelmed with work—what do you do to relax?

a. Arrange a night out with friends, partying into the early hours of the morning—it always makes you feel better.
b. Go home, put on your pajamas, and read or watch a box set on your own.
c. Phone a friend and meet for an early dinner to put the world to rights, before going home and having an early night.

Question 8

You've just been told about a new project. Do you...?

a. Like to go away and have a think before coming back into the group and talking it through with a couple of coworkers.
b. Prefer to jump straight into the action and brainstorm ideas, as you like solving problems by interacting with others.
c. Take some time to think things through and reflect on what is needed. You prefer to problem-solve by concentrating on your own.

Question 9

When traveling to work, do you prefer to commute with someone or on your own?

a. I love traveling with someone so I can talk through the day ahead or talk about the day I've just had. I don't like it to be quiet and prefer to talk things through.
b. I like to travel on my own so I can think things through before and after work.
c. Some days I prefer to be on my own and others with someone. I do like some quiet time, but also some time to talk things through to. A bit of balance.

Question 10

You've been invited to a wedding where the only people you know are the bride and groom, but because of numbers you cannot take a guest. How do you react?

a. Decline the invitation, as there is no way they'll have time for you, and it would be too awkward and tiring to make small talk for a whole day.
b. Accept, but only stay for the daytime events and leave before the evening celebrations. You're sure they'll sit you next to someone you can chat to.
c. Accept—who cares if you don't know anyone, as it's an opportunity to meet new people. You can't wait for the day to arrive.

Question 11

You've been invited out for a drink with your coworkers straight from your workplace—how do you react?

a. Agree to go for one drink and then come home, it's been a busy day.
b. You'd probably be the one arranging it and then deciding where to go onto next. It's the best way to destress at the end of the day.
c. Politely decline, as you just want to be on your own.

Question 12

Which of the following is your ideal vacation?

a. An isolated cottage near the sea with no neighbors and complete silence, on your own or with a partner or very close friend.
b. A city break with a couple of friends where you each have your own bedroom to get quiet time, but also have plenty of activities to do together.
c. A group trip with friends, with lots of fun activities to do together all day.

RESULTS:

Q1 a ■, b ✚, c ▲	Q4 a ■, b ✚, c ▲	Q7 a ✚, b ■, c ▲	Q10 a ■, b ▲, c ✚
Q2 a ▲, b ■, c ✚	Q5 a ✚, b ▲, c ■	Q8 a ▲, b ✚, c ■	Q11 a ▲, b ✚, c ■
Q3 a ✚, b ▲, c ■	Q6 a ■, b ▲, c ✚	Q9 a ✚, b ■, c ▲	Q12 a ■, b ▲, c ✚

MAINLY ■ INTROVERT

Compassionate, sensitive, and honest.

You are an introvert. This doesn't mean you are "shy," it means you get your energy from your internal world which is full of ideas and experiences, and you recharge from reflecting on your thoughts, memories, and feelings. Although you can appear to some as private and self-contained, you will take the initiative when the situation or issue is important to you. You work out your ideas by reflecting on them and direct your energy inward. When it comes to learning, you find that quiet reflection and mental practice are what works for you and you prefer to communicate in writing (email, text messages, and messenger were all made for you).

MAINLY ✚ EXTROVERT

A preference for gaining energy from the world around you.

You are an extrovert. This doesn't mean in the "gregarious" sense of the word; it just means you tend to prefer focusing your energy on the outer world, where it involves people and activity. So, what does this look like? You'll direct your energies outward and you'll receive your energy from taking direct action, as well as preferring to receive energy socializing and interacting with others. You are probably quite sociable and are very attuned to your surrounding environment. You work through ideas by talking and you prefer to communicate on the phone or face to face, rather than by email, text, or any other written form. This is also your preference for learning—you learn best by doing and by discussion.

MAINLY ▲ AMBIVERT

A preference for a balance of gaining energy from your internal world and from the world around you.

You may be an ambivert, i.e. someone who sits in the middle of extrovert and introvert. Many people find they are in the middle and this is OK. Equally, over the years you may have learnt that the world is an extroverted world and adapted your behavior accordingly to fit in. This will have been subconscious, and you probably aren't even aware of doing it. What you do know is that as much as you like getting your energy from your outer world, you need time away as well to recharge. Our preference for extroversion and introversion develops in the first part of our life, and we develop a balance of these preferences as we get older. You may be at an age where you have integrated your preference for extroversion and your non-preference for introversion, or vice versa. We learn from each other, and one preference is no better than another.

2

WHAT IS YOUR COLOR PERSONALITY?

When we think of colors, we automatically associate them with certain traits. A red car means speed. A yellow sunflower we associate with being happy. If you asked someone what color they would associate with you, I am sure most people could answer straight away. So what color are you? How does that reflect in your personality? Is this the color you'd associate with yourself? Over the following pages you'll be able to answer some questions and discover your color personality.

Insights Discovery®

This test has been inspired by Insights Discovery®. The Insights Discovery® system is a psychometric tool based on the theories of psychologist Carl Jung. It was developed by father-and -son team of Andi and Andy Lothian in Scotland in the late 1980s.

The Insights Discovery® system is a powerful framework for self-understanding and understanding others, and helps individuals to make the most of the relationships that impact them in the workplace. It uses a simple visual four-color model to help people understand their own strengths and what they bring to the team they work in. These are called the color energies—Fiery Red, Sunshine Yellow, Earth Green, and Cool Blue—and it's this unique mix which determines how and why people behave in the way they do.

To give the following type preferences:

Director (red): Decisive, self-reliant, courageous
Motivator (orange): Assertive, dynamic, enthusiastic
Inspirer (yellow): Sociable, optimistic, expressive
Helper (lime green): Engaging, encouraging, empathetic
Supporter (green): Caring, cooperative, patient
Coordinator (turquoise): Thoughtful, diplomatic, dependable
Observer (blue): Consistent, precise, organized
Reformer (purple): Self-disciplined, dedicated, pragmatic

Please go to the resources section (see page 142) to find out more on Insights Discovery®.

Question 1

What is your favorite flower?

a. Sunflower.
b. Red rose.
c. Bluebell.
d. Snowdrop.

Question 2

Where is your favorite place for a weekend break?

a. Somewhere by the sea with a loved one.
b. A vibrant city break where you can go to a show with friends.
c. A trip to the countryside with someone close.
d. Somewhere hot and sunny with family.

Question 3

What do you like to do on your day off?

a. Shopping and socializing.
b. Spend time outdoors.
c. Spend time with friends and family.
d. Sleep.

Question 4

What warm drink would you like right now and where would you drink it?

a. Tea in a café or hotel.
b. Hot chocolate, curled up with a book.
c. Coffee in a trendy bar.
d. Herb or fruit tea, sat in the backyard.

Question 5

What are you most likely to do if you find you are out and don't have your phone?

a. People watch.
b. Start a conversation with someone.
c. Take in your surroundings.
d. Daydream.

Question 6

What is your favorite view?

a. The night sky.
b. A beautiful sunrise or sunset.
c. A city skyline lit up at night.
d. Woodland.

Question 7

What job would you hate to do?

a. Accountant.
b. Working in a factory.
c. Mail delivery driver.
d. Doctor.

Question 8

What really annoys you?

a. Loud noise.
b. Indecision.
c. Close-mindedness.
d. Rudeness.

Question 9

Do you find it easy to make friends?

a. Very easy, I have lots of friends.
b. Easy if we have a common interest or connection.
c. I find it really hard, but when I make a connection it lasts.
d. I struggle.

Question 10

Where in your home do you spend most of your time?

a. In the backyard or somewhere outside.
b. The kitchen.
c. The lounge.
d. Your bedroom.

Question 11

If you were to pick a new hobby what would it be?

a. Playing an instrument.
b. Gardening.
c. A new dance class.
d. Painting.

Question 12

Which season do you prefer?

a. Spring.
b. Summer.
c. Fall.
d. Winter.

RESULTS:

Q1 a ■, b ✚, c ▲, d ★	Q4 a ■, b ▲, c ✚, d ★	Q7 a ✚, b ★, c ■, d ▲	Q10 a ★, b ✚, c ■, d ▲
Q2 a ▲, b ✚, c ★, d ■	Q5 a ■, b ✚, c ★, d ▲	Q8 a ★, b ✚, c ■, d ▲	Q11 a ■, b ★, c ✚, d ▲
Q3 a ✚, b ★, c ■, d ▲	Q6 a ▲, b ■, c ✚, d ★	Q9 a ✚, b ■, c ★, d ▲	Q12 a ■, b ✚, c ★, d ▲

MAINLY ✚ BRIGHT RED
Bold, assertive, loves excitement.

You love life and getting to know people. You thrive on being the center of attention and are a social animal. You are often seen as the life of the party, and how people regard you is very important to you. You are ambitious and like to get things done, and have real drive to achieve your goals and dreams. You will tell people exactly what you think and don't hold back in getting your point across. Being seen, being heard, and being the person people admire and look to is what you desire most.

MAINLY ★ EMERALD GREEN
Serene, accommodating, passionate about your values.

You are the outdoors type, always wanting to get into nature and explore the world in your own quiet way. You value harmony and prefer to avoid conflict where you can, but if someone does something against your values, then you will passionately defend them. You know that being in nature recharges your batteries, and that being with people too much can drain you. You are always looking for meaning, for a cause that is close to you which is congruent with your values and beliefs. Being known as the caring, passionate person is what makes you feel good.

MAINLY ■ SUNFLOWER YELLOW
Optimistic, nurturing, and friendly.

Family and friends are important to you, but although you like spending time with them you aren't a big party animal and prefer smaller events where you can chat with everyone. You always look on the bright side and see the best in people, and you love deeply. Everyone thinks of you as the happy, caring person who always looks for the positives in life. You like to feel part of an extended family, whether at home or in the workplace. Community is an essential part of your being and one where you feel whole and complete.

MAINLY ▲ SKY BLUE
Dependable, quiet, thoughtful.

You like time on your own to re-energize but also to think through each decision to ensure that the right choices are being made, which means some people think you spend too much time in your head, but this is how you manage the world around you. You value honesty and are relaxed about life, but also understand the importance of doing what you should when you said you would do it. You are always there for the people you love, but tend to prefer to do this on a one-to-one basis rather than in a large crowd.

3

WHAT IS YOUR CONFLICT TYPE?

Conflict—there are some people who thrive on it, and some people who avoid it at all costs. Then there are others who would prefer not to deal with conflict, but acknowledge it's something they need to resolve to move forward in life. In this test you'll identify your conflict preference and those of the people around you, so that you can find ways to bridge the communication gap and turn conflict into amicable resolutions.

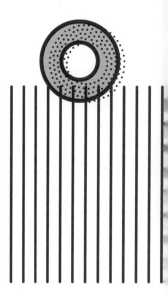

The Enneagram®

This test has been inspired by The Enneagram® (pronounced "any-a-gram"), a psychological system with roots in sacred tradition. It maps out the nine fundamental personality types of human nature and their complex interrelationships. It was pulled together by Oscar Ichazo, who was based in South America.

The symbol of the Enneagram® is a tool for personal development and transformation. It shows you how you can overcome your inner barriers, realize your unique gifts and strengths, and discover your deepest direction in life. It can be used to improve relationships, let go of bad habits, and increase personal awareness by giving insights into the deepest emotions, fears, and desires of each type. The nine personality types are:

1. The Reformer: principled and idealistic.
2. The Helper: caring and interpersonal.
3. The Achiever: adaptable and success-orientated.
4. The Individualist: romantic and introspective.
5. The Investigator: intense and cerebral.
6. The Loyalist: committed and security-orientated.
7. The Enthusiast: busy and productive.
8. The Challenger: powerful and dominating.
9. The Peacemaker: easy-going and self-effacing.

Please go to the resources section (see page 142) to find out more on The Enneagram®.

Question 1
When it comes to a conflict situation...

a. You aim for a give-and-take approach.
b. You want to get across your point so that the other party understands it.
c. You try to keep conversations civil and everyone happy.

Question 2
To resolve an argument...

a. You will meet halfway for a resolution.
b. You will accommodate other people's preferences.
c. You'll argue your case strongly.

Question 3
In times of conflict...

a. You always try and steer the conversation to positive things.
b. You keep things factual and avoid bringing in emotion.
c. You try to keep quiet, as you dislike the stress of the situation.

Question 4
In times where you cannot come to an agreement...

a. You are calm and collected and will try to find a solution for all.
b. You get the issues raised and discussed and will make the decision yourself if no one else will.
c. You will defer it to everyone else.

Question 5
You find conflict situations...

a. Stressful, they make you anxious.
b. You enjoy the challenge.
c. You like to look at all sides of the situation.

Question 6
Who do you find normally instigates conflict?

a. You do, you love a heated debate.
b. If it's something you think is important or if it clashes with your values, you will react.
c. You'd never instigate conflict.

Question 7
In an argument, what do you do?

a. Ask questions to calm the situation and make everyone happy.
b. Keep quiet.
c. Strongly point out your thoughts to resolve it asap.

Question 8
If someone is gossiping about someone you respect, you...

a. Walk away.
b. Challenge them and tell them it is wrong.
c. Try to get them to see that person from your viewpoint.

Question 9
When making a joint purchase with a friend, you...

a. Tell them what you want, you've made your decision.
b. List their requirements and your requirements and make a joint decision.
c. Listen to what they want and go with that.

Question 10
If you see someone being abusive to a friend or coworker...

a. You walk away embarrassed, you're sure they wouldn't want you to have seen.
b. You barge in and start shouting at the other person, protecting your friend.
c. You go over and ask if they need any help.

Question 11
If you discover you haven't been invited to an event, what do you do?

a. You tell everyone how disappointed you are and make it clear you won't invite them to your events.
b. You assume they have a legitimate reason and just leave it.
c. You call them and and ask if it was an oversight or if they are limiting numbers.

Question 12
If someone is making negative comments about you...

a. You take them to one side and tell them how it makes you feel, but ask them what you can do to make them see you differently.
b. You challenge them openly and think of lots of negative things to say about them.
c. You hope that it will go away.

RESULTS: ?

Q1 a 2, b 3, c 1	Q4 a 2, b 3, c 1	Q7 a 2, b 1, c 3	Q10 a 1, b 3, c 2
Q2 a 2, b 1, c 3	Q5 a 1, b 3, c 2	Q8 a 1, b 3, c 2	Q11 a 3, b 1, c 2
Q3 a 2, b 3, c 1	Q6 a 3, b 2, c 1	Q9 a 3, b 2, c 1	Q12 a 3, b 2, c 1

25-36 BULLDOZER

You know what you want and aren't afraid of conflict.

You thrive on conflict and know how to get your position heard. To some, your way of dealing with problems can seem quite aggressive and you may harm others either verbally or physically. Sometimes you create conflict for the fun of it and struggle to understand why others take it so personally. You believe it's best to get everything out in the open and that being "devil's advocate" to provoke a response is a great way of finding new ideas, and getting things sorted. It's all about getting a balance of ensuring you don't avoid a discussion, but also listen to the other opinions to get a balanced viewpoint.

13-24 PEACEKEEPER

You like to give everyone a voice and find an amicable solution.

You believe every conflict situation can be resolved with discussion. You try to find solutions to problems and deal with things in a healthy and positive way. You express your own opinions confidently, but also listen to others as well. When a conflict situation arises, you will attempt to see the viewpoint of everyone involved, using language to try to please everyone in order to reach an amicable solution. Sometimes, though, you are conscious the larger characters who thrive on conflict can still take the lead and you can find it hard on occasions to avoid going along with their viewpoint simply to keep the peace.

1-12 AVOIDER

You try to avoid all conflict.

You tend to avoid problems and do nothing rather than trying to resolve conflict. You often feel frustrated at not being heard, though you find the thought of standing up for your values quite daunting and intimidating. In a conflict situation your natural response is to hide and run, or just give in so you can avoid the discussion. But over time this constant avoidance strategy leads you to feel more and more unhappy. In turn, this results in you becoming stressed and eventually dealing with a conflict situation with an emotionally charged outburst. Try looking for small areas where you can express what you want, rather than avoiding conflict.

4

WHAT KIND OF ASTRONAUT ARE YOU?

We all had dreams of what we wanted to be when we were children and some of you, I am sure, imagined becoming an astronaut and flying to the moon. What we tend to forget is that there are many different skills needed to venture into space, so this light-hearted test allows you to determine what type of astronaut you could be, and even to make your own crew with your family and friends.

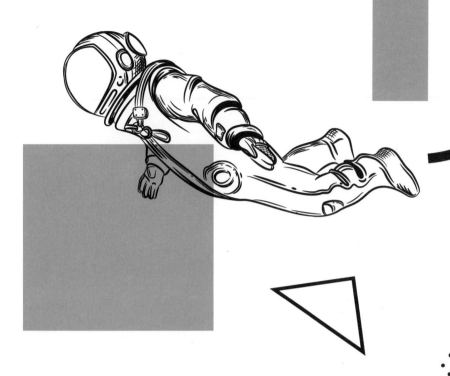

The Process Communication Model® (PCM)

This test was inspired by The Process Communication Model® (PCM), which helps to identify the communication preferences of individuals. It was developed by US psychologist Dr. Talbi Kahler, and was used by NASA between 1978 and 1996 for astronauts embarking on space missions.

For NASA, the most important aspect of PCM was that it could accurately predict how astronauts would react under pressure. In more general settings, this test can provide individuals with the tools to understand and analyze conflict and miscommunication, enabling them to find ways to resolve any issues to improve communications. The PCM model groups people into six personality types:

1. Thinker: exceptional in organizing activities and detailed planning.
2. Persister: a person who sees the world through the filters of their values and beliefs.
3. Harmonizer: a warm, compassionate person who sees the world through the filter of feeling.
4. Rebel: a creative person who finds solutions in situations when others see only problems.
5. Imaginer: an introspective and imaginative person.
6. Promoter: a charming and likeable person.

Please go to the resources section (see page 142) to find out more on The Process Communication Model®.

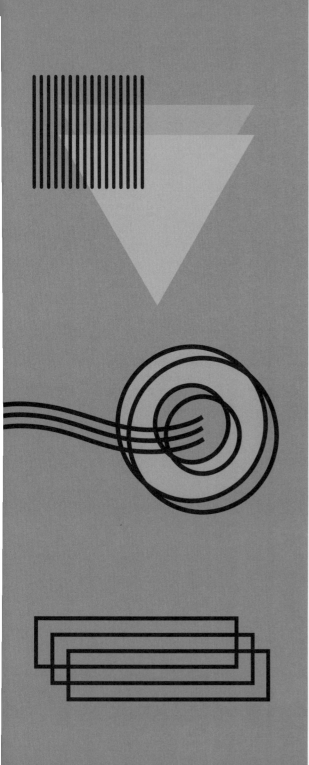

Question 1
As a child, when you looked at the stars, what did you think?

a. You thought they are so pretty.
b. You wondered if there is life out there.
c. You wanted to go out there and explore them.
d. You wanted to learn all about them.

Question 2
Do you think man really landed on the moon or was it a cover-up?

a. Yes, man landed on the moon, it's an amazing achievement.
b. Yes, but you think there is something they aren't telling us, and you want to know more.
c. Yes, most probably, but you're amazed they got there on such low-tech equipment.
d. You think it's a cover-up, as too many things don't make sense.

Question 3
Which were your favorite subjects at school/college?

a. Biology, chemistry, psychology.
b. Math, physics, engineering.
c. Business studies, geography, art.
d. Sports, politics, sciences.

Question 4
Which of the following was your dream job growing up?

a. Something where I earn loads of money.
b. Director of a company.
c. Engineer.
d. Scientist.

Question 5

You come across an accident, what do you do?

a. Phone the emergency service and assess the situation, then instruct people what to do.
b. Find the person in charge and ask them what you can do.
c. Identify where support is needed and go and help.
d. Go past, there are plenty of people there and you don't want to get involved, but you do tell everyone you know what happened.

Question 6

What roles did you play in school or college?

a. Running the science team events.
b. Sports captain.
c. Fixing up bicycles, cars, and motorbikes.
d. The joker who was always finding ways to make a bit of cash on the side.

Question 7

What do you do to unwind at the end of the day?

a. A meal with close family where you ensure everyone has a good time.
b. Party with friends.
c. Read your latest science journal with a hot drink.
d. Fix something.

Question 8

In a team, are you...?

a. The doer.
b. The organizer.
c. The leader.
d. The idea's person.

Question 9

What word sums you up the best?

a. Curious.
b. Driven.
c. Entrepreneur.
d. Problem-solver.

Question 10

You are made redundant from your job, what do you do?

a. You are sad and frustrated, but accept the decision and know you will get another job.
b. Set up your own business as you've been looking for an opportunity for a change.
c. You volunteered as you knew the situation and what would work best for the company. You understand sacrifices need to be made.
d. Take all the training and advice they offer and then look for a new job.

Question 11

Do you believe in aliens?

a. Yes, although you think it could be some form of artificial intelligence.
b. There is most probably some form of life in the universe, but you don't think it would take a human form.
c. At this time there is no evidence when you look at the information in front of you now, although this could change in the future.
d. Yes, I can't wait to meet them, as long as they aren't like those ones in the movies who always seem to want to kill us.

Question 12

Which is your favorite space craft?

a. Apollo 11, used in the moon landing.
b. The International Space Station.
c. The Space Shuttles.
d. The Virgin Galactica—it'll be amazing when built.

MAINLY ■ COMMANDER

Responsible for overall mission success, safety of crew, and the Space Station.

You are the person everyone can rely on, they come to you for advice, for guidance, and they know that you will always point them in the right direction. Confident and assertive under pressure, you know how to bring people on the journey. You look out for everyone and ensure that everyone comes together as a team. When difficult decisions need to be made, you can make them, whilst understanding the implications to everyone involved. You understand that sometimes sacrifices need to be made to deliver the overall goal.

MAINLY ✚ FLIGHT ENGINEER

Responsible for overall mission success, engineering and controls, science support.

You are the person everyone needs in their team, the person who quietly and confidently gets stuff done. You will look at every aspect to find the solution and make the appropriate decisions to achieve the end result. As long as you are given clear tasks and goals, then you are happy to proceed and work at your own pace to help deliver the overall objective. You don't particularly like to do the leadership-type roles, but are the essential support that every great leader needs. You like to brainstorm ideas on your own first, but then share them with the wider team.

MAINLY ▲ SCIENCE OFFICER

Primary responsibility for station's science experiments.

You are all about identifying patterns and prefer to work on your own, analyzing and processing to find logical outcomes. There are so many unknowns and you are looking for the answers. Whether that is the logic of how something evolves to interactions between objects, people, the world around you. Everything is linked—"does a butterfly flapping its wings in the rainforest really cause a tornado in the USA?". You are able to look out and see the bigger picture whilst being able to zoom back into the detail to find the answers that are needed. You are always on the lookout for the next big idea.

MAINLY ★ SPACEFLIGHT PARTICIPANT

Space tourist, you are coming along for the ride.

You love life and want to explore it all, take the photos, wear the t-shirt, be the first to visit places, and tell your story. Life is an adventure where you want to have fun, it's too short to be serious, that's for others. You work to live, rather than live to work, but you know that to achieve all of your dreams you need to have ambition and drive to make it happen. And you always do. Your focus on positivity means you manifest everything you want in life and generally experience it fully.

5

WHAT IS YOUR COMMUNICATIONS PREFERENCE?

Have you ever noticed how some people seem to take in information in a different way to you? Whatever your communication preference, knowing what it is can really help you to communicate better with others, as well as with learning, developing, communication, and even selling. Do the test on the following pages to find your preference.

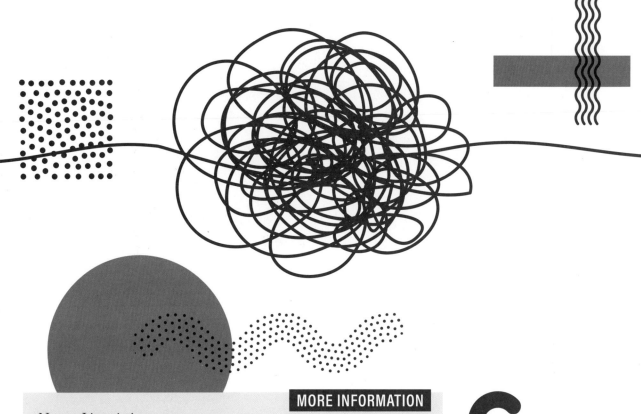

Neuro-Linguistic
Programming ® (NLP)

This test is inspired by the NLP Communication Model. Neuro-Linguistic Programming® (NLP) began as a model of how we communicate and interact with ourselves and others. It explains how we process the information that comes in from outside us and what we do with it inside. It was developed by John Grinder and Richard Bandler.

Our minds take in and process about two million pieces of information per second. The unconscious mind filters this information so that it's more manageable and many studies (conducted in the 1950s) suggest that this filtering takes it down to a manageable seven bits of information per second (+/- 2). One of the key things to understand is our preference for taking in information and communicating. We receive information into our system via our five senses—what we see, hear, feel/touch, taste, and smell. In NLP the VAK (visual, auditory, kinesthetic) test allows you to determine your preference for receiving information and communicating. This test groups people into four categories:

Visual (V): a preference for seeing.
Auditory (A): a preference for hearing.
Kinesthetic (K): a preference for touching and feeling.
Auditory Digital (AD): a preference for logic and data.

Please go to the resources section (see page 142) to find out more on Neuro-Linguistic Programming®.

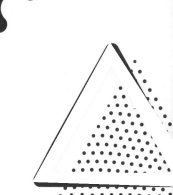

This is a short test to define your preferred representational system, or to put it in simpler terms, it relates to how we think and process information and experiences. For each of the following statements, place a number by every phrase, using the following system to indicate your preference (note you can use a number only once). Go with the first answer that pops into your mind as this gives the best indications.

4 gives the best description of you.
3 is the next best description of you.
2 is the next best description of you (compared to 3).
1 is the least descriptive of you.

Answer quickly and honestly; there are no right or wrong answers.

Question 1
You've an important decision to make— what do you base it on?

a. Gut feeling and intuition. ____
b. What sounds best. ____
c. What looks best. ____
d. The most logical option, after a review and study of the issues. ____

Question 2
During a discussion, you are most likely to be influenced by:

a. What the person is saying and their tone of voice. ____
b. Whether you can or can't see the other person's point of view. ____
c. The logic of the person's argument on this topic. ____
d. What you feel about the person's argument. ____

Question 3
You easily communicate what is going on with you by:

a. How you look. ____
b. What feelings you share. ____
c. How you choose your words. ____
d. The tone of your voice. ____

Question 4
You find it easiest to:

a. Find the ideal volume and tuning on my music player. ____
b. Select the most intellectually relevant point in an interesting topic. ____
c. Select furniture that is comfortable. ____
d. Select color combinations for a room. ____

Question 5
Which best describes you?

a. I'm sensitive to the sounds around me. ____
b. I make sense of new facts and data. ____
c. I'm sensitive to how clothing feels on my body. ____
d. I respond strongly to colors and to how a room looks. ____

Question 6
Which statement do you relate to the most strongly?

a. I can hear what you're saying. ____
b. That makes sense to me. ____
c. That looks right. ____
d. That feels good. ____

Question 7
When choosing a house, what do you consider first?

a. How it feels when I enter the house and how I'll feel living in it. _____

b. How much it will cost to heat, light, etc. _____

c. The look of the house and the area it's within. _____

d. How much noise there is from roads, neighbors, etc. _____

Question 8
What best describes you at a presentation?

a. I feel I'm in touch with the presenter, the material is easy to grasp. _____

b. There is a visual display so I can visualize the content. _____

c. It's logically presented with facts and figures. _____

d. Sound is clear, the presenter speaks clearly with a variety of tonality. _____

Question 9
When on vacation, what's the best description for you?

a. This vacation makes sense due to the cost, location, etc. _____

b. The color of the water, the sky, the sun shining brightly, the scenery. _____

c. The feel of the sand, the breeze on my face, the warmth of the sun. _____

d. The whistle of the wind, the birds, and the roar of the waves. _____

Question 10
You experience change when:

a. Things begin to feel different. _____

b. Things start to look different. _____

c. Things start to make or not make sense. _____

d. Things begin to sound different. _____

Question 11
You are starting a new project—which statement do you relate to?

a. I see what needs to be done. _____

b. I can make sense of the new facts and data. _____

c. I hear what needs to be done. _____

d. I can feel what I need to do. _____

Question 12
There is an important announcement:

a. I can see the big picture. _____

b. I hear what they are saying, I can talk or listen to get more information. _____

c. I can get in touch with what is happening here. _____

d. I can make sense of these things in my head. _____

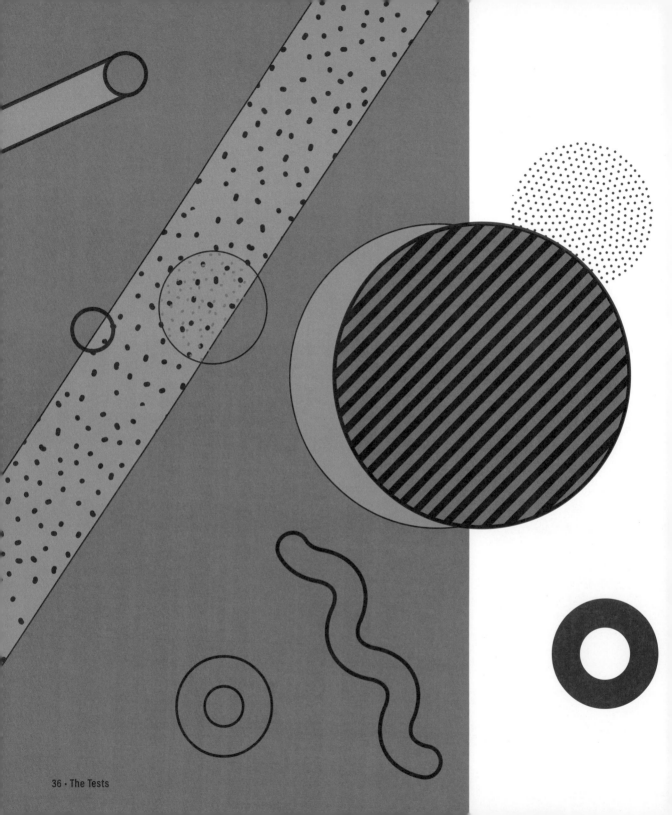

RESULTS:

For each of the questions note your answers in the space next to the appropriate letter, for example, if you gave Question 1, option d, 4 points, then you would write 4 next to d in the chart below. The total scores in each column will give the relative preference for each of the four major representational systems. The one with the highest score is your preference, but you will use the other preferences too and within your scores you'll determine which are your next preferred communication types.

1	c ___	b ___	a ___	d ___
2	b ___	a ___	d ___	c ___
3	a ___	d ___	b ___	c ___
4	d ___	a ___	c ___	b ___
5	d ___	a ___	c ___	b ___
6	c ___	a ___	d ___	b ___
7	c ___	d ___	a ___	b ___
8	b ___	d ___	a ___	c ___
9	b ___	d ___	c ___	a ___
10	b ___	d ___	a ___	c ___
11	a ___	c ___	d ___	b ___
12	a ___	b ___	c ___	d ___
Total	Seeing ___	Hearing ___	Feeling ___	Logic ___

SEEING
You are a visual person.

You prefer to take in information in a visual form, whether that is it is written down, in pictures, or looking at the world around you. You may notice you use words such as "I see what you mean," "I can visualize that," "I'd like to see the bigger picture." When learning or taking in information, you prefer images, videos, and colors to help you to understand what needs to be done. Although you like words, you do prefer them to be broken up with images too.

HEARING
You are a hearing person.

You prefer to take in information through sound, you like to listen and to talk things through. You may notice you use phrases such as "I hear what you are saying," "That sounds good," "I'm not sure I like the sound of that," "That rings true to me." As you are sensitive to sound, you may be drawn to podcasts and audiobooks as a way of learning and to help you think and process your thoughts.

FEELING
You are a feeling person.

You prefer to take in information through sensations such as touch and holding things. You learn by interacting with things and can find presentations hard to follow, often you'll end up playing with a pen, eating cookies, holding a cup—anything to keep your hands busy and get you interacting with your feeling preference. You'll find you are sensitive to how things feel to your touch and how your clothes feel when you put them on. You may find you use phrases like "I can't put my finger on it," "It feels right to me," "It's taking me a while to grasp that concept."

LOGIC
You are a logical person.

You prefer to get the facts and process the data to understand what is happening. You learn by research and understanding the information presented in front of you. If it doesn't make sense, you need more data and more facts. You are the person in a presentation who wants all of the data behind it— you aren't bothered about it looking good, you just want data. You may find you use phrases such as "I understand you," "That's logical." You'll be drawn to in-depth text to develop your learning.

6 ARE YOU NEUROTIC OR STABLE?

The word neurotic is often seen as a negative trait, but all of us suffer some form of neurosis in our lives. Where we are on the scale is what matters and understanding this can help individuals look for help in the right places. On the following pages you can find out where you sit on the scale, bringing an understanding of how you can support yourself and others.

The Eysenck Personality® Inventory (EPQ)

This test has been inspired by The Eysenck Personality® Inventory (EPI), which was developed in 1964 by Hans and Sybil Eysenck to measure the two broad personality-type dimensions of Extraversion-Introversion and Neuroticism-Stability. It was developed from Hans' interest in the Greek humors (or temperaments)—Sanguine, Choleric, Phlegmatic, and Melancholy.

The EPI is considered a relatively simplistic self-reporting instrument and comprises 57 yes/no items that produce total scores for extraversion and neuroticism, as well as a validity score (e.g. Lie Scale). People who do the test are classified as "high" or "low" on these two dimensions. The "Lie Scale" is scored out of nine. It measures how socially desirable you are trying to be in your answers. Those who score five or more on this scale are probably trying to make themselves look good and are not being totally honest in their responses, which is always a problem with any test that is done.

Extraversion: seen as social, carefree, and optimistic.
Introversion: seen as quiet, introspective, and reserved.
Neuroticism: prone to emotional distress and instability.
Stable: generally calm and emotionally stable.

Please go to the resources section (see page 142) to find out more on The Eysenck Personality® Inventory.

Question 1

You feel threatened by other people.

a. Strongly agree
b. Agree
c. Neither agree or disagree
d. Disagree
e. Strongly disagree

Question 2

You go to sleep every night worrying.

a. Strongly agree
b. Agree
c. Neither agree or disagree
d. Disagree
e. Strongly disagree

Question 3

You get easily panicked.

a. Strongly agree
b. Agree
c. Neither agree or disagree
d. Disagree
e. Strongly disagree

Question 4

You always fear the worst.

a. Strongly agree
b. Agree
c. Neither agree or disagree
d. Disagree
e. Strongly disagree

Question 5

You expect things to always work out how you want them to.

a. Strongly agree
b. Agree
c. Neither agree or disagree
d. Disagree
e. Strongly disagree

Question 6

You often feel optimistic and happy.

a. Strongly agree
b. Agree
c. Neither agree or disagree
d. Disagree
e. Strongly disagree

Question 7

You have frequent mood swings.

a. Strongly agree
b. Agree
c. Neither agree or disagree
d. Disagree
e. Strongly disagree

Question 8

You like how you look.

a. Strongly agree
b. Agree
c. Neither agree or disagree
d. Disagree
e. Strongly disagree

Question 9

You are often unhappy.

a. Strongly agree
b. Agree
c. Neither agree or disagree
d. Disagree
e. Strongly disagree

Question 10

You worry about things.

a. Strongly agree
b. Agree
c. Neither agree or disagree
d. Disagree
e. Strongly disagree

Question 11

You assume that any mistake is due to you.

a. Strongly agree
b. Agree
c. Neither agree or disagree
d. Disagree
e. Strongly disagree

Question 12

You believe that you can create your own future.

a. Strongly agree
b. Agree
c. Neither agree or disagree
d. Disagree
e. Strongly disagree

RESULTS:

Q1 a 5, b 4, c 3, d 2, e 1	Q4 a 5, b 4, c 3, d 2, e 1	Q7 a 5, b 4, c 3, d 2, e 1	Q10 a 5, b 4, c 3, d 2, e 1
Q2 a 5, b 4, c 3, d 2, e 1	Q5 a 1, b 2, c 3, d 4, e 5	Q8 a 1, b 2, c 3, d 4, e 5	Q11 a 5, b 4, c 3, d 2, e 1
Q3 a 5, b 4, c 3, d 2, e 1	Q6 a 1, b 2, c 3, d 4, e 5	Q9 a 5, b 4, c 3, d 2, e 1	Q12 a 1, b 2, c 3, d 4, e 5

12-28 YOUR NEUROTICISM LEVEL IS BELOW AVERAGE

You are very emotionally stable. You are always looking for the positives in life and see every challenge as something sent to teach you so that you can grow. You see life as a series of steps and only focus on things that you recognize are within your control. This emotional stability means that people find you a calming influence and you are often seen as someone who will turn any negative situation into a positive, even if for some this is irritating. You have control of your negative emotions and can manage them and know how to quickly deal with them.

29-44 YOUR NEUROTICISM LEVEL IS AVERAGE

You are less easily upset than many people and where possible try to remain upbeat and positive about most things. However, most people will experience some negative moods due to stress or events in their lives. As long as you are aware of this, you know how to get out of these cycles so that you can regain composure and make it easy to make the right decisions. Recognizing when these negative emotions are taking hold is all part of developing self-awareness and how your energy and emotions can impact others. By being aware when these negative emotions take over, you have found a way to balance them and bring you back to a positive mindset.

45-60 YOUR NEUROTICISM LEVEL IS ABOVE AVERAGE

You are someone who experiences high levels of negative feelings, such as anxiety, fear, anger, sadness, hurt, and guilt. It may be that it is one of these emotions in particular that impacts you the most, but because of this you find you respond to events in a much more emotionally negative way than other people. Your reactions often seem more intense than normal and you can interpret the most minor of frustrations as hopelessly difficult. It's common for you to interpret ordinary situations as threatening. You find it hard to communicate how you feel and can appear to others as always being in a bad or low mood.

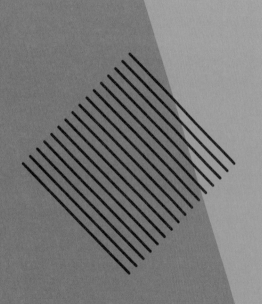

7

ARE YOU HONEST WITH YOURSELF?

In a world of social media, likes, and followers, the need to be "liked" can seem like the most important thing to consider. More and more people post images of "their life," taking snapshots of the good bits, but not sharing the boring, the mundane, or the bad bits. What we show the outside world is also often a reflection of how honest we are with ourselves. And until we can be honest with ourselves, how can we be honest with the world around us? Take the quiz on the following pages to find out how honest you are with yourself.

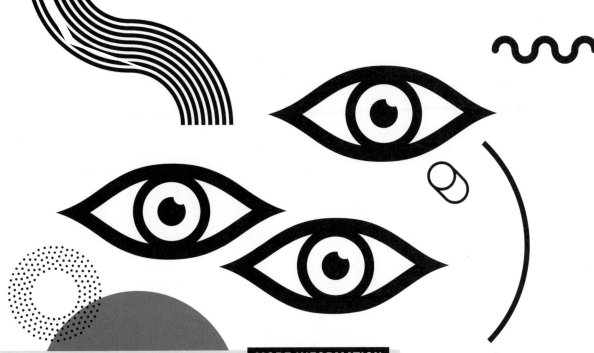

The Hexaco Model of Personality Structure Inventory®

This test has been inspired by The Hexaco Model of Personality Structure Inventory®. This began development in 2000 by Kibeom Lee Ph.D and Michael C. Ashton Ph.D. The aim of this work has been to truly test and assess personality in a modern way.

This model uses the ideas of the "Big Five Personality Factors" developed in the early 20th century, and has since discovered a sixth factor which hadn't been recognized before, that of Honesty-Humility. The six personality dimensions are:

Honesty-Humility (H): sincere, honest, faithful, loyal, modest/unassuming versus sly, deceitful, greedy, pretentious, hypocritical, boastful, pompous.
Emotionality (E): emotional, oversensitive, sentimental, fearful, anxious, vulnerable versus brave, tough, independent, self-assured, stable.
Extraversion (X): outgoing, lively, extraverted, sociable, talkative, cheerful, active versus shy, passive, withdrawn, introverted, quiet, reserved.
Agreeableness (A): patient, tolerant, peaceful, mild, agreeable, lenient, gentle versus ill-tempered, quarrelsome, stubborn, choleric.
Conscientiousness (C): organized, disciplined, diligent, careful, thorough, precise versus sloppy, negligent, reckless, lazy, irresponsible, absent-minded.
Openness to Experience (O): intellectual, creative, unconventional, innovative, ironic versus shallow, unimaginative, conventional.

Please go to the resources section (see page 142) to find out more on The Hexaco Model of Personality Structure Inventory®.

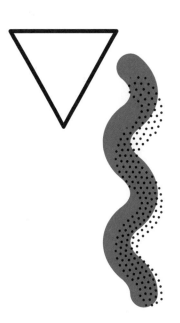

Question 1

A friend keeps messaging, saying they need to speak to you, but you know that it isn't usually important. What do you do?

a. Call later when you are less busy.
b. Phone them immediately.
c. Ignore and then tell them you were in a meeting.
d. Ignore and when you see them next, say you didn't get the text.

Question 2

You find yourself attracted to another person; would you ask them on a date?

a. Yes, the worst that can happen is they say no.
b. Ask them to meet for a drink as friends to gauge their interest.
c. No, but secretly stalk them on social media and try to find reasons to bump into them.
d. No, they are out of my league. They'd never look at me so forget about them.

Question 3

A loved one buys you a present, but you hate it. What do you do?

a. Tell them you love it and then hide it in a drawer, planning on giving it to charity one day.
b. Say thanks and keep it on display, but then accidentally break it or lose it.
c. Say you think it's faulty and can you take it back for repair or exchange, with a plan to exchange it.
d. Politely tell them it's not your thing, and ask if you can take it back to change for something else.

Question 4

You are invited on vacation to a place you really don't want to go. You...

a. Politely decline and say it's not your thing.
b. Tell them you'll get back to them as you aren't sure if you are available.
c. Say yes, but then find an excuse not to go.
d. Reluctantly say yes because you know they need the numbers.

Question 5

Your dream job is being advertised, but on reading the advert you see that you only have 50% of the criteria to apply for it. What do you do?

a. Don't apply, only having 50% of the skillset won't get you the job.
b. Lie on your CV and covering letter—you can fake it when you get the job.
c. Apply using a generic letter and hope they don't notice.
d. Apply anyway, no one is ever perfect, you have nothing to lose and be honest with them in the covering letter.

Question 6

When someone asks you what you do for work...

a. You tell them exactly what you do.
b. You downplay what you do.
c. You change the subject.
d. You make your work sound more interesting than it really is.

Question 7

You find telling the truth...

a. Usually the best thing to do but not always.
b. Something you should carefully consider before answering.
c. Something that no one ever truly does as we all have our own version of the truth.
d. Something we should always do; there is never a justified reason to lie.

Question 8

How easy do you find it to share your opinion and get yourself heard?

a. Very easy.
b. Most of the time you can.
c. It depends on the circumstances.
d. You struggle as you are not sure if your opinion counts.

Question 9

How often do you share details of your personal life with others?

a. Very often—you like to share and like to listen to others, it's important.
b. Rarely—you only share it with people really close to you.
c. Often, but only with people who share information about their personal life.
d. Never—it's none of anyone else's business.

Question 10

You choose the clothes you wear based on...

a. What you think you should wear because of your role.
b. What is in fashion, whether it suits you or not.
c. What feels most comfortable to you, you like being an individual.
d. If they will make you fade into the background.

Question 11

You are on a healthy-eating plan and you have a day where you eat unhealthily. What do you do?

a. Don't worry about it, no one is perfect.
b. Beat yourself up but return back to the healthy-eating plan and do more to balance out that day.
c. Give up for a few days, but plan to go back to it in a month.
d. Stop eating healthily and give up, you can't do it.

Question 12

If a doctor asks you how much you drink, or smoke, how do you answer?

a. You completely lie and tell them you don't.
b. You reduce them by 50%.
c. You may play the figures down a bit, but not much as sometimes that is correct.
d. Honestly, and tell them the information you have nothing to hide.

RESULTS:

Q1 a 4, b 3, c 2, d 1	Q4 a 4, b 3, c 2, d 1	Q7 a 4, b 2, c 3, d 1	Q10 a 2, b 3, c 4, d 1
Q2 a 4, b 3, c 2, d 1	Q5 a 1, b 2, c 3, d 4	Q8 a 4, b 3, c 2, d 1	Q11 a 4, b 3, c 2, d 1
Q3 a 1, b 2, c 3, d 4	Q6 a 4, b 2, c 1, d 3	Q9 a 4, b 2, c 3, d 1	Q12 a 1, b 2, c 3, d 4

12-24 BELOW AVERAGE

You lack honesty with yourself.

It's so easy to do what we think we should do rather than being true to ourselves, and you are one of those people. You are the person who lies to themself about what they eat, how much exercise they do, what they drink, etc. Yet the only person you are lying to is you. It's really hard to be honest with ourselves, but unless we are then no one will be honest to us. So start with small steps. Are you being honest? What do you need to do to be more authentic? Why do you feel you need to lie to yourself and others?

25-36 AVERAGE

You are becoming more honest with yourself.

Most people will find days when they are not honest with themselves. How many times have you been on vacation and thought about your life and how it's not what you want it to be? We have all been there.

Yet we lie to ourselves about why we "should" do something, instead of doing what is authentic and right for you. Start being a little more honest each day. And when you do this, you can find major shifts happen in your life.

37-48 ABOVE AVERAGE

You are honest and authentic with yourself.

You have grown and developed and learnt that until you are honest with how you feel, with the way you look, and what you do, then you cannot be honest with the world around you. You've learnt that being honest with yourself releases you from a burden of what you should do. When you are honest with yourself, you can recognize your strengths, development opportunities, and true potential. You can control your fears and take control of what is within your sphere of influence, and with it you can create a life that is authentic for you.

8

ARE YOU SPONTANEOUS OR A PLANNER?

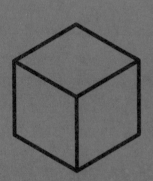

Some people naturally seem to plan everything down to the minutest detail, whilst others like to be spontaneous and go with the flow. As you can imagine, you can be anywhere on this scale and the more extreme you are, the more likely it is that you cannot understand the other person's point of view. In the following test you can determine your preference, and with it there is a short exercise to help you understand more about those with a different preference to you.

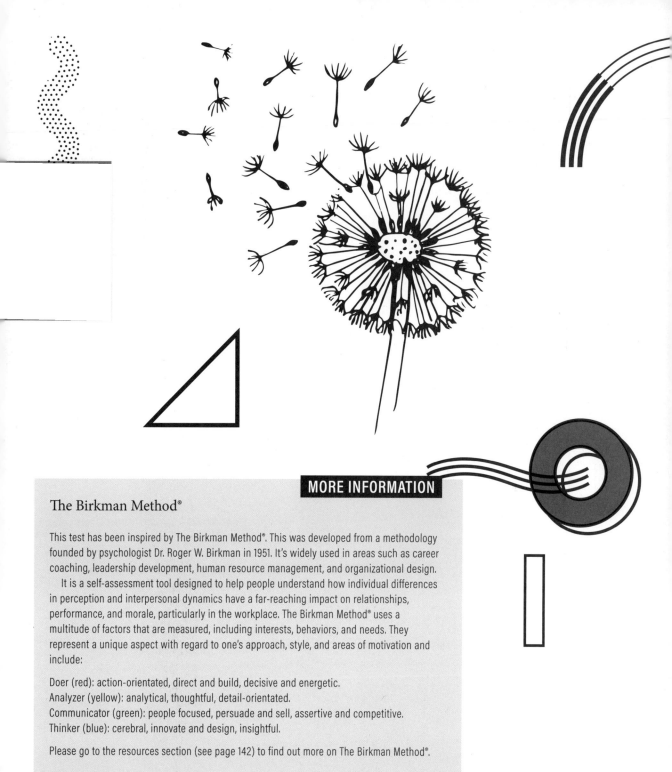

The Birkman Method®

This test has been inspired by The Birkman Method®. This was developed from a methodology founded by psychologist Dr. Roger W. Birkman in 1951. It's widely used in areas such as career coaching, leadership development, human resource management, and organizational design.

It is a self-assessment tool designed to help people understand how individual differences in perception and interpersonal dynamics have a far-reaching impact on relationships, performance, and morale, particularly in the workplace. The Birkman Method® uses a multitude of factors that are measured, including interests, behaviors, and needs. They represent a unique aspect with regard to one's approach, style, and areas of motivation and include:

Doer (red): action-orientated, direct and build, decisive and energetic.
Analyzer (yellow): analytical, thoughtful, detail-orientated.
Communicator (green): people focused, persuade and sell, assertive and competitive.
Thinker (blue): cerebral, innovate and design, insightful.

Please go to the resources section (see page 142) to find out more on The Birkman Method®.

Question 1

You feel anxious if you don't have an itinerary for the weekend, even if it is just rest time.

a. Strongly agree
b. Agree
c. Neither agree or disagree
d. Disagree
e. Strongly disagree

Question 2

You write a list when you go shopping and only purchase what is necessary.

a. Strongly agree
b. Agree
c. Neither agree or disagree
d. Disagree
e. Strongly disagree

Question 3

You don't like it when a meeting agenda is changed at the last minute.

a. Strongly agree
b. Agree
c. Neither agree or disagree
d. Disagree
e. Strongly disagree

Question 4

When planning a vacation, you like to book well in advance.

a. Strongly agree
b. Agree
c. Neither agree or disagree
d. Disagree
e. Strongly disagree

Question 5
You work first and only do recreational activities in their allocated time after the working day.

a. Strongly agree
b. Agree
c. Neither agree or disagree
d. Disagree
e. Strongly disagree

Question 6
Freedom to do what you want, when you want, where you want is something you dream of.

a. Strongly agree
b. Agree
c. Neither agree or disagree
d. Disagree
e. Strongly disagree

Question 7
You find it easy to change your mind about an arrangement at short notice.

a. Strongly agree
b. Agree
c. Neither agree or disagree
d. Disagree
e. Strongly disagree

Question 8
You couldn't go on a blind date.

a. Strongly agree
b. Agree
c. Neither agree or disagree
d. Disagree
e. Strongly disagree

Question 9
You love a night out where you don't know where you'll go next.

a. Strongly agree
b. Agree
c. Neither agree or disagree
d. Disagree
e. Strongly disagree

Question 10
You love just getting in the car or on the train and heading anywhere without a plan.

a. Strongly agree
b. Agree
c. Neither agree or disagree
d. Disagree
e. Strongly disagree

Question 11
You hate being surprised with anything.

a. Strongly agree
b. Agree
c. Neither agree or disagree
d. Disagree
e. Strongly disagree

Question 12
You would feel comfortable leaving a job with no other job lined up.

a. Strongly agree
b. Agree
c. Neither agree or disagree
d. Disagree
e. Strongly disagree

12-28 SPONTANEOUS

You love spontaneity.

You love just getting up and going with no plans and no idea where you are headed. You dislike routine and staying in one place for long periods of time. Going on a detailed, planned vacation with an itinerary laid out for you would be your idea of a nightmare. For you working in a standard 9-to-5 job is not what energizes you, you want flexibility to be spontaneous and you handle change well. There is an assumption that spontaneous people can't deliver as they are too flighty and dislike working to constraints and deadlines. But in the right sort of environment you can flourish, and you need to determine what that is for you. If you are in an overly planned environment for too long you can find it frustrating and draining, so finding some way to break the monotony is key for you. Working with planners can be hard for you to comprehend.

29-44 BALANCED

You know when to have fun and when to plan.

You recognize the benefits of planning and of being a bit more spontaneous. Some things need a plan and you may have learnt how to do this to become more effective, some things you like to just go with the flow. Most of us have a preference over one than the other, but as we develop we can find ways to gain the skills of both. When you are working on something that is highly scheduled and where you have planned it out, if you operate in this environment for a long time do you find it energizing or draining? If you find it energizing then you may lean more toward being a planner, but if you find it draining you may lean more toward being spontaneous.

45-60 PLANNER

You love to have a plan and an itinerary.

You are someone who likes to know exactly what you are doing at what time every day. You don't like surprises and dislike change that happens at short notice. If anyone needs something planning and organizing, then you will be the one with lists and details with exact timings on what to do. You find people who have a preference toward spontaneity frustrating and assume that they can't get things done if they don't operate in the same way as you. In a work situation this can often cause a clash as you may perceive these people to be unfocused and they may be distracting to you.

OPTIONAL FUN EXERCISE

Take your group or team or family and let's see who is a planner and who is more spontaneous.

Ask the question: Do you like to work first and then play? Or do you prefer to play, then work? Or are you in-between.

Ask people to stand in a line. Those on the left-hand side will be the ones who like to play first or play when they want, who like to be spontaneous with their day. Those on the right-hand side will be those who like to plan and have an itinerary. Then there will be some in the middle, some right in the middle who are a balance of both, and some more toward play first and some more toward work first.

Now ask the people on the right-hand side to explain what is frustrating about people on the left-hand side. And then ask people on the left-hand side to explain what is frustrating about people on the right-hand side. Keep it fun, as it's a great way to get to know one another.

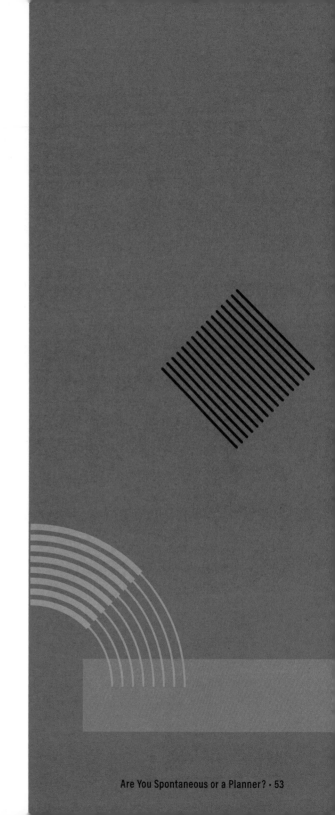

9

WHAT IS YOUR EMOTIONAL INTELLIGENCE LEVEL?

You've probably heard the term emotional intelligence, but it can be difficult to understand how it applies to you. Knowing where you fit on the emotional intelligence scale can help you to recognize your development opportunities, and on the following pages you'll find where you fit. Understanding it can help us to move forward to success in a way that fits better with our own values and beliefs.

Emotional Intelligence

This test is inspired by the research and developments on Emotional Intelligence (EI). This is defined as the ability to not only understand and manage your own emotions, but also the emotions of others. It was first defined in a 1964 paper by Michael Beldoch and a 1966 paper by B. Leuner.

It became popular after the release of Daniel Goleman's book *Emotional Intelligence: Why it can matter more than IQ*, in 1995. People with a high degree of EI understand what they are feeling and why. They understand their own emotions and how these emotions can impact others, but also how to motivate themselves and others too. Many models of EI have been developed over the years. A common model claims that EI includes four types of abilities:

1. Perceiving emotions: the ability to recognize and understand emotions in faces, pictures, and voices, including the ability to identify one's own emotions.
2. Using emotions: the ability to harness emotions to facilitate thinking and problem-solving.
3. Understanding emotions: the ability to comprehend emotion language and to appreciate complicated relationships among emotions.
4. Managing emotions: the ability to regulate emotions in both ourselves and in others.

Please go to the resources section (see page 142) to find out more about Emotional Intelligence.

Question 1

I can understand what people are feeling by listening to the sound of their voice and their mannerisms.

a. Strongly agree
b. Agree
c. Neither agree or disagree
d. Disagree
e. Strongly disagree

Question 2

When I have to deal with a challenge, I give up because it is too hard.

a. Strongly agree
b. Agree
c. Neither agree or disagree
d. Disagree
e. Strongly disagree

Question 3

I always let people know that I appreciate them if they've done something well.

a. Strongly agree
b. Agree
c. Neither agree or disagree
d. Disagree
e. Strongly disagree

Question 4

I always look for the positives in life.

a. Strongly agree
b. Agree
c. Neither agree or disagree
d. Disagree
e. Strongly disagree

Question 5

I sometimes struggle knowing when it's appropriate to speak to people about my personal worries.

a. Strongly agree
b. Agree
c. Neither agree or disagree
d. Disagree
e. Strongly disagree

Question 6

There have been some major events in my life and it has made me realize what is and isn't important to me.

a. Strongly agree
b. Agree
c. Neither agree or disagree
d. Disagree
e. Strongly disagree

Question 7

My emotions control me, I don't have control over them at all.

a. Strongly agree
b. Agree
c. Neither agree or disagree
d. Disagree
e. Strongly disagree

Question 8

I like helping other people if they are feeling sad.

a. Strongly agree
b. Agree
c. Neither agree or disagree
d. Disagree
e. Strongly disagree

Question 9

I can't tell what other people are feeling when I look at them.

a. Strongly agree
b. Agree
c. Neither agree or disagree
d. Disagree
e. Strongly disagree

Question 10

When someone tells me about something important to them, I can feel it as though it were as important to me.

a. Strongly agree
b. Agree
c. Neither agree or disagree
d. Disagree
e. Strongly disagree

Question 11

I look for activities that make me happy.

a. Strongly agree
b. Agree
c. Neither agree or disagree
d. Disagree
e. Strongly disagree

Question 12

I find it hard to understand the non-verbal messages of other people.

a. Strongly agree
b. Agree
c. Neither agree or disagree
d. Disagree
e. Strongly disagree

RESULTS:

Q1 a 5, b 4, c 3, d 2, e 1	Q4 a 5, b 4, c 3, d 2, e 1	Q7 a 1, b 2, c 3, d 4, e 5	Q10 a 5, b 4, c 3, d 2, e 1
Q2 a 1, b 2, c 3, d 4, e 5	Q5 a 1, b 2, c 3, d 4, e 5	Q8 a 5, b 4, c 3, d 2, e 1	Q11 a 5, b 4, c 3, d 2, e 1
Q3 a 5, b 4, c 3, d 2, e 1	Q6 a 5, b 4, c 3, d 2, e 1	Q9 a 1, b 2, c 3, d 4, e 5	Q12 a 1, b 2, c 3, d 4, e 5

12-28 YOUR EMOTIONAL INTELLIGENCE LEVEL IS BELOW AVERAGE

You are probably one of those people who can get overwhelmed, especially in stressful situations, and because of this you tend to avoid conflict situations, even though you know that resolving them would make things better. When you feel upset, you can find your emotions run wild and you over analyze and relive the event over and over again. All of this can make it difficult for you to find connection with the right people and build strong working relationships. However, all is not lost—now you know this, you can look at things that will help you.

29-44 YOUR EMOTIONAL INTELLIGENCE LEVEL IS AVERAGE

You've developed a level of emotional intelligence that gets you through most of the time and generally you can cope with your emotions and have good relationships with people. However, you probably find that you still have some people you struggle with, who you find really difficult and who seem to trigger you. When this happens you probably kick yourself and wish that it hadn't happened, but you recognize this and because of that you are able to take steps to develop yourself to cope better in the future. Look at the people or things that trigger you and find ways to review the angers that arise, so you can step back and make more considered, less emotionally charged responses.

45-60 YOUR EMOTIONAL INTELLIGENCE LEVEL IS ABOVE AVERAGE

People like you often have great leadership potential. You are a good listener and you probably find that people often come to you for advice, or just to chat things through. Not surprisingly you will have great relationships with others, but you also have to be careful that you aren't constantly giving to them and not fulfilling your own needs. Look for every opportunity for you to continue to develop and grow. With this level of emotional intelligence it's also great to help transfer your knowledge to bring people up to the same level as you, which not only enhances your growth and development, but theirs too.

10

ARE YOU A LEADER OR A FOLLOWER?

Not everyone wants to lead and be seen; equally, not everyone wants to follow the crowds and some of us find that it often depends on our circumstances. If it's something we are truly passionate about we may want to take the lead and in other instances, follow. Over the following pages you can determine what your preference is and recognize when is the best time for you to lead and when you should follow.

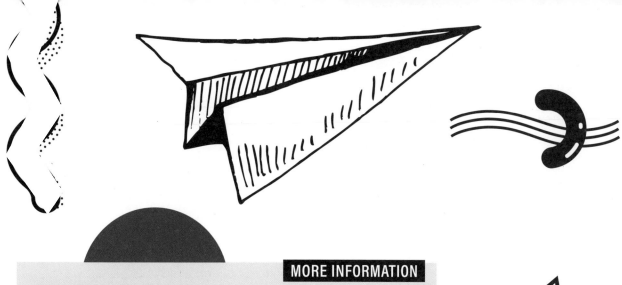

Hogan Personality Inventory®, Development Survey, Motives, Values, and Preference Inventory

This test has been inspired by the Hogan Personality Inventory®, which was developed by Drs. Joyce and Robert Hogan in 1987. It's a tool used to help organizations strengthen employee selection, leadership development, succession planning, and talent management. It's a measure of day-to-day personality and is known as the bright-side.

Employers use this assessment to determine how well you work with others, how you lead or follow, and if you are successful in certain positions. It's based on the Five-Factor Model of personality. There are two scales you are measured on.

Primary scale

Adjustment: confidence, self-esteem, composure.
Ambition: initiative, competitiveness, desire for leadership.
Sociability: extroversion, gregariousness, need for social interaction.
Interpersonal sensitivity: tact, perceptiveness, ability to maintain relationships.
Prudence: self-discipline, responsibility, conscientiousness.
Inquisitive: imagination, curiosity, creativity.
Learning approach: achievement-orientated, stays up to date on business and technical matters.

Occupational scale

Service orientation: attentive, pleasant, courteous.
Stress tolerance: able to handle stress, even-tempered.
Reliability: honesty, integrity, positivity.
Clerical potential: ability to follow directions, pay attention to detail, communicate clearly.
Sales potential: energy, social skills, the ability to solve problems.
Managerial potential: leadership ability, planning, decision-making skills.

Please go to the resources section (see page 142) to find out more about The Hogan Personality Inventory®.

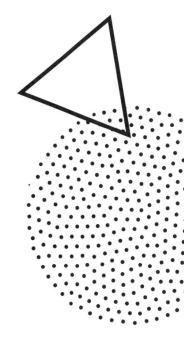

Question 1
A local community project is organizing an event—what part do you play?

a. I will be the one leading it from the start as without me I know it won't happen.
b. I'll be working away in the background.
c. I often start working away in the background, but then find people start gravitating to me for direction.

Question 2
Being a responsible leader who doesn't let power go to their heads is...

a. How every good leader should operate.
b. A lovely idea, but it's never implemented.
c. Not realistic, the world needs people who just take control and make decisions.

Question 3
How do other people see you?

a. A born leader.
b. A good team player.
c. A good leader who cares.

Question 4
Someone accuses you of being power crazy—how do you react?

a. Surprised, but then look at the situation and recognize in that instance perhaps you were.
b. Thank them, you know you are and it's why you are good at what you do.
c. Feel horrified, you'd never want anyone thinking of you like this and quickly address the issue.

Question 5

Which do you think is most important— being liked or being powerful?

a. Having a balance, it's easier if everyone can work together in harmony but it's not always possible.
b. You don't have to be liked to be a leader, you need to get the job done and that might mean most people don't like you for it.
c. Being liked.

Question 6

You are on jury duty and you have got to pick a foreman—how do you react?

a. If no one else will do it, you will, but it's a big responsibility.
b. Loudly tell everyone that you will do it and want to be nominated, as you really don't think anyone else in the room is capable.
c. Try and make yourself as small as possible and hope you don't get nominated.

Question 7

Two project teams have been merged together—how do you manage this?

a. Tell everyone you will be leading, and you will continue to do things how they were being done in your team and the other team needs to follow suit.
b. Hope someone is going to tell you how this is going to work.
c. Ask everyone's opinions of how they feel about the situation and how they think it should work.

Question 8

Volunteers have been asked to attend leadership training—what do you do?

a. Volunteer immediately.
b. Switch off as soon as you hear the word "leadership" and get back to work.
c. You'll go if someone asks you to.

Question 9

When a member of your team is promoted to a new position which is level with yours, how do you feel?

a. Angry, they can't possibly be at that level yet.
b. Excited, you've been tutoring and mentoring them and so glad to see them grow.
c. Happy for them, it's nice to see people in the organization getting promoted, though it's not for you.

Question 10

At work, if you had a choice, what would you feel most comfortable wearing?

a. The company uniform—it's easy, you know you're wearing what is appropriate, and it's one less thing to think about.
b. A tailored suit to show everyone your status in the organization.
c. Something smart and comfortable which shows your individuality but also demonstrates you are professional.

Question 11

What would you be prepared to do to climb the leadership ladder?

a. I feel I should do something and find people are always asking me to take the next step, but I'm not sure.
b. Nothing, it doesn't interest me.
c. Whatever it takes.

Question 12

You are invited to a team-building activity—how do you feel?

a. Nervous, and wonder if you can get out of it, worried they'll make you lead a task.
b. Excited, you love these events and to take the lead in the activities.
c. No need to worry until the day, when you'll take the role that is required depending on what the task is.

RESULTS:

Q1 a +, b ▲, c ■	Q4 a ■, b +, c ▲	Q7 a +, b ▲, c ■	Q10 a ▲, b +, c ■
Q2 a ■, b ▲, c +	Q5 a ■, b +, c ▲	Q8 a +, b ▲, c ■	Q11 a ■, b ▲, c +
Q3 a +, b ▲, c ■	Q6 a ■, b +, c ▲	Q9 a +, b ■, c ▲	Q12 a ▲, b +, c ■

MOSTLY + YOU ARE A DRIVEN LEADER
You are ambitious and will deliver whatever the cost.

You know you have the drive and determination to get things done and you find that most people just don't know what to do. You find it easier for you to tell people and direct people as you know everyone needs clear direction. If they aren't happy with that, then they are in the wrong place. Being in charge is where you feel happiest and you often get frustrated at others' lack of competence. You will do whatever it takes to climb the career ladder and that might mean upsetting people on the way. You want the power to tell people how to do things.

MOSTLY ■ YOU ARE A NATURAL LEADER
You don't like the limelight; you lead when you need to.

You step into whatever role is right at the time. Often working away in the background, you find that people gravitate to you for direction. You like to listen to everyone's viewpoint and hope that you can guide them in the right way. Often you find others nominating you to take the lead, even when you hadn't planned on doing it. On other occasions you acknowledge you are probably the best person to lead but aim to train and develop someone to do this going forward. If you are in a room where there are too many leaders, you will step back as a follower.

MOSTLY ▲ YOU ARE A FOLLOWER
Being a follower isn't a bad thing.

It's easy to think that being a follower is a weak thing. Followers are the ones that get stuff done, the key workers who can often be overlooked. But every leader needs the followers to deliver what is required. Look at nature and the example of a worker bee reporting to their queen. The follower role is as important as the leader role and you are destined to play an important part in whatever activity you are involved in. Recognizing that this is your position is a good thing, as you know what makes you happy and for you going into a leadership role would make you stressed. Often in organizations everyone is being driven to have career aspirations, yet some are just happy doing the day-to-day tasks with small development opportunities in their current role.

11

WHAT IS YOUR RELATIONSHIP TO MONEY?

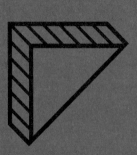

Money can often be one of the things we struggle to talk about, and each of us has our own thoughts and behaviors about money. In the coming pages we'll look at your money personality and how understanding it can help you with your relationship with your finances. Perhaps you are someone who is a saver, or perhaps you are a spender? Understanding why you interact with money in the way that you do can really change your money mindset and open up new opportunities for you.

Sacred Money Archetype®

This test is inspired by Sacred Money Archetypes® (SMA), an assessment model developed by business coach Kendall Summerhawk, to help entrepreneurs to understand their relationship with money and with it discover their unique money code so that they can become successful.

Many people have a difficult relationship with money and can fear facing up to these insecurities. The SMA tools are used by coaches to help individuals break through and understand their money relationships, how to clear money block, how to embrace their money strength and gifts, and how to manage their money challenges. From the assessment individuals will discover their top three Archetypes of the Eight Sacred Money Archetypes®:

Ruler: your inner empire builder.
Accumulator: your inner banker.
Connector: your inner relationship creator.
Alchemist: your inner idealist.
Maverick: your inner rebel without a cause.
Celebrity: your inner big shot.
Nurturer: your inner sponsor.
Romantic: your inner hedonist.

Please go to the resources section (see page 142) to find out more on Sacred Money Archetypes®.

Question 1

Your cellphone needs replacing as it has a damaged screen and is at the end of its contract—what do you do?

a. Go out and purchase the most up-to-date model that is available—you want the latest technology and aren't worried about the cost.

b. Spend as much time as possible researching all the options for renewing your contract and whether to purchase a new phone or a refurbished phone—you will make this phone last as long as possible and can tape it together if necessary.

c. Look at what you need now, and what you can get for a similar price to your existing contract. You need a phone, but it doesn't need to be the newest version.

Question 2

You've just received a massive bonus at work—what do you do?

a. Treat yourself to one thing you really want and put the rest into savings or paying off debts.

b. Invest it all into your pension.

c. Plan a weekend of shopping, you've been working so hard it's time to enjoy it.

Question 3

You are going shopping, do you...

a. Make a list of everything you need, research which stores stock these items, check prices online, and then determine the most effective way to go around and get the items at the best price.

b. Check how much money you have available on your credit cards, then go and explore to see what you find—you love shopping.

c. Set yourself a budget for what you can spend that day, having in mind what you think you actually need, but you don't have to be rigid about it.

Question 4

You are invited to a wedding which is some distance away so would require an overnight stay. What do you do?

a. Book the most expensive suite in the wedding hotel and choose some treatments in the spa to prepare for the wedding, plus it's a great time to buy a whole new outfit.

b. Decide to go but only for the day and leave early so you don't have the cost of an overnight stay. You'll dig something out of your closet to wear.

c. You look forward to it, but stay in a cheaper hotel close to the wedding venue. Perhaps buy some new accessories to update a current outfit.

Question 5

Your new year's resolution is to get fit—what do you do?

a. Buy new sportswear, new trainers, and sign up for a 12-month membership to the latest trendy gym (knowing full well you will probably only use the members' bar).

b. Dig out your sportswear and sign up for some taster sessions at your local sports center to determine what is right for you.

c. Dig out your old trainers and sports clothing and start going for a daily run.

Question 6

You have just been paid—how do you deal with your finances?

a. Pay your bills, pay off debts, invest and save, buy what you need.

b. Pay your bills, invest and save, you have no debts, determine if there are any essentials you need and put money aside for them.

c. Do some shopping and/or organize a big night out with friends.

Question 7
You are planning a vacation for a special occasion, do you...?

a. Look at your savings, determine what you can afford taking into consideration all of the costs, and book what will fit your budget.

b. You want to make this a special event and go somewhere you'll remember, so you'll use some savings and charge some expenses to your credit card with a plan of how you'll pay it off beforehand.

c. Find your dream destination and resort—this is a special occasion so you'll celebrate it in style with all the add-ons and a new wardrobe of clothes. You can put it on the credit card. You only live once.

Question 8
Your friends call to organize a last-minute night out, but it's end of the month and you've used up your budget. Do you...?

a. Suggest a night in with takeout food at your house, as you know everyone else will be feeling the pinch too.

b. Decline, you don't have the money and you can go out another time when you do have some.

c. Get out the credit card, you've had a mad month and need some fun; you'll pay it off next month.

Question 9
At work, what do you do for lunch?

a. Sometimes I take lunch and I treat myself every so often to a bought lunch.

b. Go out to a local restaurant or café with coworkers.

c. I always take my own lunch that I make at home.

Question 10
It's time to do you grocery shop, do you...?

a. Make a detailed list of all your meals for the week, check what ingredients you have, and then purchase only what you need.

b. Turn up at the store and buy anything, then when you get home order a takeout as you can't be bothered to cook.

c. Have an idea of what you want to cook, but check the sale items first, you'll make up something from what you find.

Question 11
You are looking for somewhere new to live and find your dream property, but it is out of your price range. Do you...?

a. Put in an offer, you'll figure something out regarding how to pay for it.

b. Look at ways you can earn another income to get it, such as renting out a room, or getting another job, or selling something.

c. It's out of your price range, so look for something smaller in a different area that is better suited to your budget.

Question 12
You suddenly get an unexpected bill— what do you do?

a. Take money from your emergency fund, this is what it is for.

b. Pay for some of it from savings and some on credit card. You weren't expecting it and it caught you out, but that's why you have credit cards as a backup.

c. Panic, your credit cards are maxed out, so you start determining who you can borrow some money from.

12-19 FRUGAL

You only spend what you must.

Your money relationship is all about saving, but this can also be at the expense of having fun. You avoid taking risks and if you haven't got the money, you won't purchase it. You tend to make do and mend and want to ensure you have lots of savings for your retirement. It's great that you watch your money so much, but do remember to live a little and that it's OK to dream and aspire for more. Perhaps start a "fun money" account, even just a small amount put aside to spend on things to live a bit more in the moment, to enjoy life now.

20-27 SAVVY SAVER/SPENDER

You live life.

Life is for living, but you also know that you have to be cautious with your money too and have enough to cope with life's eventualities. Although you save and try to plan, you also want to enjoy life now as you don't know what will happen in the future. This is a healthy relationship to have and means you can enjoy life with the security of knowing you are also planning for the future. Your money mindset gives you the freedom you require without constraining you to not living in the here and now.

28-36 HEY BIG SPENDER

You live for the moment.

You love life and see spending as a way to treat yourself for all your hard work. As soon as the money comes in, you have either already spent it or are thinking of how to spend it. You have no savings, but you are worrying about how to pay off those debts and bills all the time. Look at your money relationship and see what is it that makes you spend money without thinking of the future. It's good to have fun, but often when people spend with abandon it can come from underlying emotions or from a need for validation or to deal with life's ups and downs.

12

ARE YOU A PSYCHOPATH?

Do you think that some people you know have psychopathic tendencies? Perhaps you've noticed some things you do yourself and wonder if you are a little bit of a psychopath? All of us will show some tendencies toward psychopath behavior, especially under stress. Here, you can find out where you fit on the psychopath scale, from very high to low. Answer as honestly as you can and then turn to the following page to get your answer.

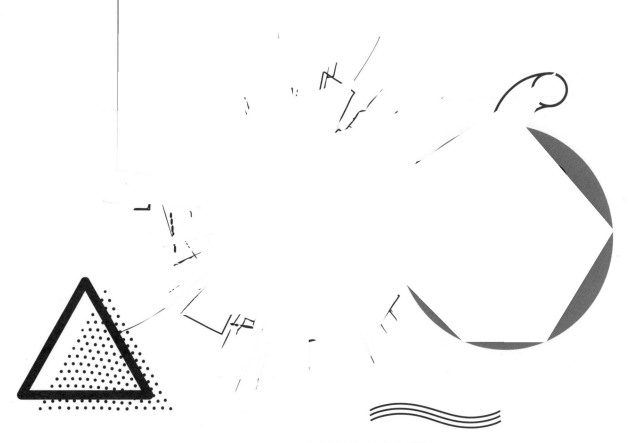

Psychopaths

Psychopathy is generally considered a personality disorder characterized by certain behaviors. The term was first used by German psychiatrists in the 19th century and originally it just meant that an individual had a mental disorder.

Since that time, the term has developed, initially to cover any person who did not conform to legal or moral expectations, or who was just generally socially undesirable. Now it is a general term for people who persistently behave in antisocial ways, lack empathy and remorse, are bold and disinhibited, and have egotistical traits. However, as psychological advances have increased, it is recognized that some people with typical psychopathic traits can learn how to manage them in order to think differently. Some research has indicated many top CEOs and leaders have many psychopathic traits but when leveraged in the right way this can lead to success. In the book *The Good Psychopath Guide to Success* by Dr. Kevin Dutton and Andy McNab, an SAS hero, they discuss how to use your inner psychopath to get the most out of life.

Please go to the resources section (see page 142) to find out more on the psychology of psychopathy.

Question 1
When the world is falling apart, you are the one...

a. Who is calm and collected, you don't know what the fuss is about.
b. Dealing with it on a minute-by-minute basis as best as you can.
c. In a mad panic.

Question 2
Could you ever physically hurt someone?

a. If the circumstances needed me too, then I would, e.g. in self-defense.
b. Yes, I would have no regrets.
c. No, I could never do that, even in self-defense.

Question 3
How do you feel about lying?

a. Sometimes you have to tell the odd white lie.
b. It's totally wrong and I'd never do it.
c. I have no problem with lying.

Question 4
Do you like extreme activities such as bungee jumping, skydiving, driving fast cars?

a. No, I hate all of that—it scares me.
b. Sometimes, it depends on what it is.
c. I love it.

Question 5
If something goes wrong?

a. It's not my fault.
b. I'll help to fix the problem.
c. I'll assume it was me.

Question 6
You apply for a promotion and a friend applies for it too—what do you do?

a. If the job is right for me, I'll get it but if it's not, then I am happy for them.
b. Do everything you can to walk all over them, so you get the role.
c. Automatically assume they will get the job or even pull out of the application process.

Question 7
Would you sleep with someone to get what you wanted?

a. Never.
b. I don't think so, but the situation has never arisen so I might.
c. Yes.

Question 8
Would you ever consider cheating at a test or an exam?

a. Possibly, it depends on what it was.
b. Never.
c. Yes, no problem.

Question 9
How would you feel about seeing an animal injured and in pain?

a. Devastated, I hate seeing animals suffer.
b. I wouldn't feel anything, it's just an animal.
c. If it was my pet I'd be upset, but if an animal in nature or one I didn't know I'd be sad, but it wouldn't keep me awake at night.

Question 10
Do you like doing things spur of the moment?

a. Not really, but I can cope with it.
b. Sometimes it's fun.
c. Yes.

Question 11
A person leaves their cash in the ATM in front of you—what do you do?

a. Wait a moment, the machine will probably pull it back in if it's not been taken. And if it doesn't, then hand the money into the bank.
b. Pocket it—it's their loss and stupidity.
c. Take the money and chase after them to hand it to them.

Question 12
Do you ever feel afraid?

a. Yes, I jump at the slightest thing.
b. In some circumstances but not all.
c. Never.

Remember that we will all exhibit some psychopathic tendencies throughout our life, whether as part of our normal personality preferences or during times of stress or learned behaviors. Sometimes these tendencies can help us to move forward in life, so check out your score below and see where you sit on the psychopath scale.

30–36 VERY HIGH
You are a psychopath.

This doesn't mean you are the next serial killer; it means you are someone who knows what they want in life and won't let anything stop them from getting it. You demonstrate many of the personality traits associated with being a psychopath (such as ruthlessness, self-confidence, lack of fear, being impulsive, being charismatic, overall mental toughness) and you probably lack empathy and a conscience. By recognizing this, you can teach yourself to have more empathy or get a friend or loved one to give a different viewpoint on a situation so that you can see it through the eyes of others. You can be a good psychopath, too.

21–29 HIGH
You show some psychopathic tendencies.

You have a high score, because you know that sometimes you need to get things done and sometimes you need to recognize when to back off. You may have a few of the traits of a psychopath, but you know how to dial them up and down as the situation arises. You may be at this point because you've watched others succeed and have mimicked their behaviors so that you can achieve your goals, but be cautious. Empathy for others is a real skill and getting a more balanced viewpoint can help you succeed as well.

11–20 AVERAGE
You are realistic about the world.

You recognize the world is not black and white, and although you are generally conscientious and want to play by the rules and work with others, when the time arises you will do what has to be done to achieve your goals, even if this sometimes makes you feel a bit uncomfortable. Knowing how to balance the wants and needs of the world around you with your value and belief systems is key. This will stop you going higher up the scoring on psychopathy but also ensure you don't shy away from the difficult decisions.

3–10 LOW
You are risk averse and prefer to avoid conflict.

You are a conscientious soul who will avoid conflict at all costs. You want to ensure that the thoughts and feelings of everyone are taken into consideration, even though this might leave you disadvantaged. You are probably highly empathetic to the world around you and can be sensitive to hurtful comments. We all have to deal with uncomfortable situations, and developing skills around confrontation and resilience will help you to find the world a little easier to live in.

13

WHAT IS YOUR STRESS TYPE?

Everyone deals with stress on a daily basis—some of it is tiny stressors, some of it is major stress, but each of us will deal with it differently depending on our preferences for coping with the world around us and with other people. In this test you'll discover your stress level and knowing this will allow you to find ways to respond in a better way, so you are in control of your stress, not your stress controlling you.

Stress

Stress is a physical, mental, or emotional issue that causes tension within our body and/or impacts our mental health. Stresses can come from a number of sources, but fit into two main categories—stress caused by factors external to you and stress caused by factors internal to you.

Over the last century there has been a lot of scientific study into the psychology of stress, which has deepened our knowledge and understanding of how stress impacts people's daily lives. This research is allowing us to understand how the mind and body react to stress, and how individuals react to different stresses in different ways. In turn, this means more appropriate advice is available on coping and developing methods for dealing with it. Stress has effects beyond the individual, and how one person copes with their stress can impact others greatly. Learning to recognize your stress response, and understanding how to cope with it, helps individuals to minimize their impact on others, so that decisions and actions can be undertaken once the stress threat has been managed.

Please go to the resources section (see page 142) to find out more on stress.

Question 1

How often do you feel difficulties are piling up so high that you cannot overcome them?

a. Never
b. Almost never
c. Sometimes
d. Fairly often
e. Very often

Question 2

How often do you feel that you are unable to control the important things in your life?

a. Never
b. Almost never
c. Sometimes
d. Fairly often
e. Very often

Question 3

How often do you find yourself holding tension in your body, such as clenching your hands or hunched shoulders?

a. Never
b. Almost never
c. Sometimes
d. Fairly often
e. Very often

Question 4

How often do you feel stressed because of something that happened unexpectedly?

a. Never
b. Almost never
c. Sometimes
d. Fairly often
e. Very often

Question 5

How often do you actively do something to reduce stress in your life?

a. Never
b. Almost never
c. Sometimes
d. Fairly often
e. Very often

Question 6

How often have you felt that things were going right for you?

a. Never
b. Almost never
c. Sometimes
d. Fairly often
e. Very often

Question 7

How often do you feel confident about handling your personal problems?

a. Never
b. Almost never
c. Sometimes
d. Fairly often
e. Very often

Question 8

How often do you feel you can't cope with all you have to do?

a. Never
b. Almost never
c. Sometimes
d. Fairly often
e. Very often

Question 9

How often are you angered because of things that happened that were outside of your control?

a. Never
b. Almost never
c. Sometimes
d. Fairly often
e. Very often

Question 10

How often do you feel anxious and stressed?

a. Never
b. Almost never
c. Sometimes
d. Fairly often
e. Very often

Question 11

How often do you feel that you are coping well with life?

a. Never
b. Almost never
c. Sometimes
d. Fairly often
e. Very often

Question 12

How often have you been able to control irritations in your life?

a. Never
b. Almost never
c. Sometimes
d. Fairly often
e. Very often

RESULTS:

Q1 a 1, b 2, c 3, d 4, e 5	Q4 a 1, b 2, c 3, d 4, e 5	Q7 a 5, b 4, c 3, d 2, e 1	Q10 a 1, b 2, c 3, d 4, e 5
Q2 a 1, b 2, c 3, d 4, e 5	Q5 a 5, b 4, c 3, d 2, e 1	Q8 a 1, b 2, c 3, d 4, e 5	Q11 a 5, b 4, c 3, d 2, e 1
Q3 a 1, b 2, c 3, d 4, e 5	Q6 a 5, b 4, c 3, d 2, e 1	Q9 a 1, b 2, c 3, d 4, e 5	Q12 a 5, b 4, c 3, d 2, e 1

12-28 TRANQUIL SOUL
You've found your inner serenity.

You take life as it comes and have an inner calm that can be sensed by everyone around you. You focus on what is within your sphere of influence and let go of tension to ensure you are not thrown off balance. Others can burn themselves out by trying to control everything, but you know the best way for you is to let go and be confident in your own way of being. You like to contemplate life, but can easily be knocked off kilter by doing stuff all the time, which really increases your stress levels. To deal with stresses in life, you need a way to stay grounded and prevent the stress of the world dominating you. By staying rooted and connected in yourself using meditation, mindfulness, daily walks, or whatever suits you, you can keep centered and ride the storm of any stressful situation.

29-44 HASSLED HEART
You take on too much.

You are always the one who follows their heart and wants to help everyone, often taking on too much. You often put elements of self-care for you on hold because you feel you need to support and help others. Generally, you handle stress quite well, but you don't always know when to say no. Your love of helping others means you always think you can take on one more thing and eventually you reach burnout, often in dramatic style. But you rarely learn and once recovered, you go back to exactly the way you were before. It's time to make some small changes in your life. Start by looking at your to-do list and delegating one thing to someone else and deciding not to do one thing. Now use this time for you. It can feel selfish at first, but having a weekly hot soak in a bath, a ride on your bike, or a walk near your home can all help you to recharge your depleted batteries, which in turn allows you to make better judgments and reduce your overall stress.

45-60 STRESS HEAD
You often feel worried.

You are the worrier, but not just normal levels of worry—you have made worrying an Olympic sport and it is now a chronic problem for you. You honestly believe everyone and everything are against you and that no one can have a life worse than yours. Even the tiniest of difficulties unsettles you and you dislike surprises or anything in your life changing without prior warning and a lot of notice. You are always displaying the signs of stress, often without a particular reason. Your stress is generally due to focusing on future problems that may not even exist, but you have already considered all of them and assume they will happen to you. To help you stop worrying you need distractions—finding a hobby where you need to focus, such as playing an instrument, painting, or cooking can help draw your mind away from your day-to-day worries. Focusing on your breath and noticing where you hold it, such as in your stomach or your chest, can help you attune with your body. But most of all, seeking help from friends or professionals to get you out of the cycle is something you should consider.

14

ARE YOU AN OPTIMIST OR A PESSIMIST?

Do you see the glass half full or half empty? Some of us are generally more positive than others and it can be difficult to understand the viewpoint of those whose preference is opposite to you. If you have a friend who is always pessimistic, you may find them draining to be with, but equally someone who is the eternal optimist can drive people mad, too. In the following test you can discover which you are and get insights into things you can do to be mindful of your impact on others and the world around you.

Positive Thinking

The power of positive thinking is being recognized across all areas of life as something that can really help people, not only mentally and physically but also to gain more success in their lives.

There's a lot of research being conducted into the impact of thinking in a more positive way. Things such as the placebo effect are attributed to people believing that this is going to work and with it, it helps them to improve their health. Although research isn't certain of why thinking positively has such an impact, it is attributed to many well-being benefits, including:

- Lower rates of anxiety and depression
- Better mental and physical health
- Better coping skills during hardships and times of stress
- Better resistance to illness and infections
- Living longer

Many top entrepreneurs attribute their success to positive thinking and more people are looking at ways to be more positive in their everyday lives. Some personalities are more prone to negative thinking than others, but we can all review our preferences and learn new skills, such as positive thinking.

Please go to the resources section (see page 142) to find out more on positive thinking.

Question 1

You've planned to go camping on the weekend, but the weather forecast says it's going to rain—what do you do?

a. Cancel, there is no point going if it's going to rain.
b. Still go, but change to a trailer or cabin; you always have a backup plan.
c. Keep everything as planned, as you're sure it will amount to nothing.

Question 2

You are running a bit late for an appointment—what do you do?

a. Relax, you are sure that you'll still make it in time.
b. Blame everyone and everything around you for the fact you are going to be late.
c. Start trying to find an alternative route to save some time.

Question 3

Do you buy lottery tickets?

a. Sometimes, but I don't expect to win.
b. Yes, because someone has to win.
c. No, it's a waste of money.

Question 4

A new housing development is being built behind your home. How do you react?

a. You are sure it will be fine and once the building work is done, life will return to normal.
b. Arrange to move to a new house, you know it will be a disaster.
c. Do some research and if there are concerns, appeal against the planning application.

Question 5

Is the glass half empty or is the glass half full?

a. Half empty is the only answer; you don't know why the question is even asked.
b. Everyone is missing the point—the glass is refillable.
c. Half full, always look for the positive.

Question 6

What do you think of your work?

a. I love what I do.
b. It is something I have to do to pay the bills.
c. It allows me to do the things that I love out of work.

Question 7

You meet your friend at a café for coffee, but when you get there you find there is a long queue to get served. What do you do?

a. Try to calculate how long it will take before making a decision.
b. Leave and go to another café as this queue will take ages.
c. Join the line, you're sure it won't take long.

Question 8

You come down with an illness which means you may have to cancel a vacation with friends—what do you do?

a. Still plan to go, you know you'll be better soon.
b. See if you can postpone or cancel; you'll have a mini vacation at home instead and ask them to send you photos.
c. Cancel, it's pointless going if you aren't well.

Question 9
Do you do anything to help the environment?

a. I try to, but I determine what will have the biggest impact.
b. Yes, every day, even if it's little things like switching off the lights—every bit makes a difference.
c. No, it's a waste of time, you can't make a difference.

Question 10
A friend loses their job— how do you respond when they phone you?

a. Tell them to call you if they need anything, you're not sure what to say.
b. Say it's a shame, especially as there are so few jobs out there.
c. Tell them everything happens for a reason and it means something better is coming their way.

Question 11
You have booked a summer vacation in a cottage in the countryside. What clothes do you pack?

a. Everything you could possibly need, including clothing for all seasons. Best to be prepared.
b. Summer basics with a raincoat and a sweater in case the weather changes. If it really changes you can buy things there.
c. It's summer, so summer clothing only—you know it will be fine.

Question 12
There is a big sporting event coming up and, in the office, they are placing bets on the outcome. What do you do?

a. You look at the odds and determine who gives you the best chance.
b. Bet on your favorite team, it would be disloyal to do anything else.
c. You never win anything, so no point placing a bet.

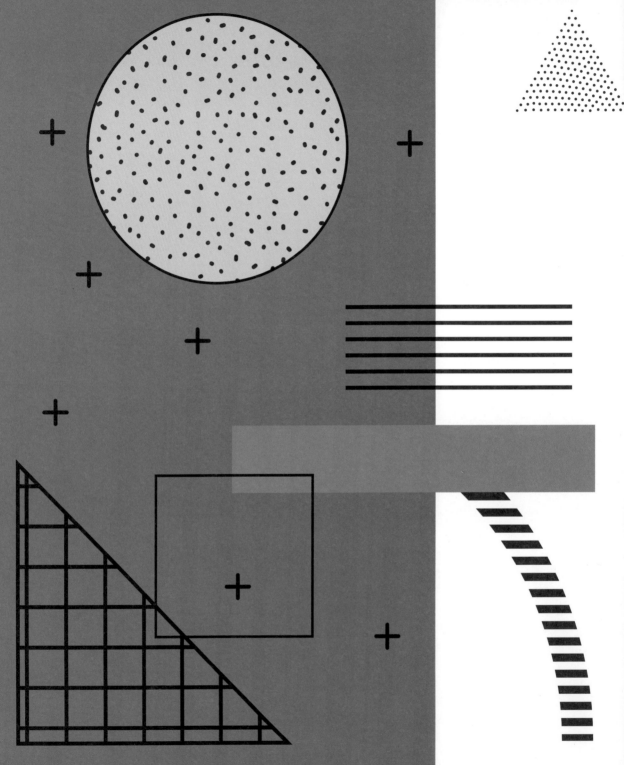

Q1 a ■, b ▲, c ✚	Q4 a ✚, b ▲, c ■	Q7 a ■, b ▲, c ✚	Q10 a ■, b ▲, c ✚
Q2 a ✚, b ▲, c ■	Q5 a ▲, b ■, c ✚	Q8 a ✚, b ■, c ▲	Q11 a ▲, b ■, c ✚
Q3 a ■, b ✚, c ▲	Q6 a ✚, b ▲, c ■	Q9 a ■, b ✚, c ▲	Q12 a ■, b ✚, c ▲

MAINLY ✚ OPTIMIST

You look for the positives and love life.

You really do look for all the positives in life and see the magic and wonder in everything. You believe that you have the power to make a positive impact in the world and that you can control the decisions and experiences that happen to you. Being a future-oriented person, you always believe that tomorrow will bring better things and see the present as something to enjoy and relish. Every event is an opportunity, every challenge is a way to learn something for the future, even if it is a negative challenge it's there to teach you something, a lesson that you need to learn. You are grateful for the little things in life and you know by recognizing that, everyday allows you to take the steps to fulfill your dreams.

MAINLY ■ REALIST

You like to remain positive, but also know that there is an element of reality.

You are the person who always has a plan and sees the world through the lens of reality. You know that bad things can happen, but if you focus on ways to mitigate the circumstances you can get the control in your life to avoid it where possible. You are always trying to anticipate what negative events could happen and what is the worst-case scenario, and then you plan how to avoid it. And with it you'll have many different plans to ensure whatever happens avoids failure. You believe that planning and hard work get you what you want in life, that there is no magic wand, and it is down to mitigation and planning to make things work out for you. You never set unreasonable expectations and keep your dreams realistic as to what it is possible to achieve.

MAINLY ▲ PESSIMIST

You assume the worst to avoid disappointment.

You always assume the worst; that way you aren't disappointed as you knew it would be bad anyway. Often you focus on the past and use that to predict your future, so if you failed at something at school, you have already decided you will fail at that for the rest of your life. You find every challenge as something sent to make your life difficult, and that because of your background you cannot achieve any more in life. You tend to take the slightest negative comment as a personal attack on you, and it just reinforces the fact that your life is already predetermined to be awful. And should a small adverse issue occur at the start of your day, you will look out for every other negative incident to prove the day is against you. Pessimists can easily become prone to depression if left to focus on the negatives in life, and even when something good happens, you will generally find something bad in the situation. To break the negative cycle, consider: 1) Find things that make you happy and focus on them; 2) Focus on solutions; 3) Change your perspective; 4) Surround yourself with optimism; 5) Give yourself compliments. Practice this daily to break the cycle of pessimism, it's OK to be realistic, but sometimes we have to reframe the world to make changes in it.

15

WHAT IS YOUR SPIRIT ANIMAL?

Spirit animals are said to embody the characteristics of each human, helping a human to find their true path. In this fun quiz you will determine which spirit animal you are, which characteristics you share, and what you can learn from that creature. A spirit animal acts as your guide, to remind you of your path and your potential, and how to stay connected and earthed to your truth.

Spirit Animals

Spirit animals are recognized by many cultures as a way for humans to connect with a deeper part of themselves. They are one of the earliest forms of linking a symbol to a human personality.

Across history we can find the story of spirit animals woven into every culture, from the Cherokee of North America to the Vikings of Scandinavia and the Aborigines of Australia. In some ways they are one of our earliest forms of personality profiling, linking a person's qualities to an animal to help categorize them and understand them, but also using the idea to help them to develop their own characteristics. Even in modern western society we describe people by the characteristics of the creatures we share this earth with. These animal archetypes are built into our subconscious as symbols of certain behaviors that we can relate to. So, describing someone as wolf-like will automatically make you assume something about them and with this knowledge you respond to them differently than if this description hadn't been used.

Please go to the resources section (see page 142) to find out more on spirit animals.

Question 1
What is your favorite leisure activity?

a. Watching TV.
b. Reading.
c. Hiking alone.
d. Exploring new places.
e. Socializing with friends.
f. Meditation.

Question 2
What type of TV do you like to watch?

a. Historical documentaries.
b. Travel programs.
c. Comedy.
d. Sitcoms.
e. You don't watch TV.
f. News and current affairs.

Question 3
What is your favorite food and where do you like to eat it?

a. A burger at a sports event with family.
b. Seafood at an outdoor BBQ with friends.
c. A healthy salad somewhere peaceful.
d. A steak dinner in a good restaurant.
e. A sandwich on the go.
f. Sunday lunch with the family.

Question 4
What is your favorite form of exercise?

a. Soccer
b. Walking
c. Running
d. Yoga
e. Water sports
f. Don't like exercise

Question 5
What subject did you enjoy most at school?

a. Geography
b. Math
c. Sport
d. History
e. Science
f. Art

Question 6
Where would you most like to travel?

a. South America
b. Africa
c. Rome
d. Scotland
e. Hawaii
f. Yellowstone National Park

Question 7
What is your preferred non-alcoholic drink?

a. Americano
b. Espresso
c. Herb tea
d. Hot chocolate
e. Tea
f. Coke

Question 8
What is your ideal date?

a. A meal at an upmarket restaurant.
b. A classical music concert.
c. Live music at a local bar.
d. Clubbing at a night club.
e. A day doing an adventure activity.
f. Somewhere quiet where you can watch the sunset.

Question 9
How much time do you spend on social media?

a. I don't go on social media.
b. Every day but I limit my time.
c. I check in once every day.
d. I am constantly on social media.
e. I chat with friends during the evening.
f. I go on about once a month.

Question 10
Why do you go on social media?

a. I use it as a way to tell everyone what is going on with my life.
b. I use it to keep connected with family.
c. I don't use it; I think it's a waste of time.
d. I don't post anything, I just like seeing what everyone else is doing.
e. I use it to connect with people like me.
f. I use it to chat with friends.

Question 11
How do you deal with stress?

a. I chat with friends.
b. Go for a run on my own to clear my head.
c. By burying myself in facts and data.
d. I step away and look at the bigger picture.
e. By spending time with family.
f. Mindfulness and meditation or a walk in nature.

Question 12
When do you usually cry?

a. At beauty in the world, at injustice in the world.
b. Rarely do I cry, but when I do it's due to frustration.
c. Quietly on my own due to injustice to loved ones.
d. I don't cry.
e. Due to achieving a goal.
f. Laughing with friends.

Q1 a ✚, b ✳, c ■, d ★, e ▲, f ♥	Q5 a ★, b ■, c ▲, d ✚, e ✳, f ♥	Q9 a ■, b ♥, c ★, d ▲, e ✚, f ✳
Q2 a ✳, b ★, c ✚, d ▲, e ♥, f ■	Q6 a ■, b ★, c ✳, d ♥, e ▲, f ✚	Q10 a ▲, b ✳, c ■, d ★, e ♥, f ✚
Q3 a ✚, b ▲, c ♥, d ■, e ★, f ✳	Q7 a ★, b ■, c ♥, d ✚, e ✳, f ▲	Q11 a ▲, b ■, c ✳, d ★, e ✚, f ♥
Q4 a ▲, b ✚, c ■, d ♥, e ★, f ✳	Q8 a ■, b ✳, c ✚, d ▲, e ★, f ♥	Q12 a ♥, b ✳, c ✚, d ■, e ★, f ▲

MAINLY ■ TIGER

You are strong and determined.

You aren't afraid to go it alone to get to where you need to be. You are logical and decisive. You lead with a strong will and you aren't afraid to make things happen, even if that means upsetting some people. You are very confident and assert your power when you walk in the room. You are comfortable making difficult decisions and will ensure the job gets done and the goals are delivered. Be careful you don't tread on people in your desire to achieve the results at all costs, because as someone who is confident walking alone you can be prone to forgetting to bring the people with you.

MAINLY ★ EAGLE

You are free and open to possibilities.

You are an adventurer, always on the lookout for new challenges, new possibilities. You love your freedom to explore the world and are a strategic thinker who looks to the bigger picture to determine your path and your direction. You are difficult to pin down and struggle with a mundane role, you want flexibility and change in everything you do, as this is what excites you and leads you to come up with ideas to do things differently. When people try to pin you down to one role, one lifestyle, one way of doing something, you feel frustrated and can rebel by taking flight, off on another adventure. Look at ways you can have stability with freedom to give you want you desire out of life.

MAINLY ▲ DOLPHIN

You are fun and chatty.

You love to be part of the gang, having fun, and are chatty and lively—the ideal person to be part of a team and bring everyone together with laughter. You look on the bright side of life and love to socialize with friends. You have a large social circle as you make friends so easily and no one can resist your charms. Sometimes people think you don't take life seriously enough, but you are loyal, honest, and kind to everyone around you. You get stuff done, you just do it in your own way. Sometimes you can forget to "adult" and this is where you might need to partner with a friend or family member to set up ways to make the adult parts of life more fun.

MAINLY ✚ BEAR

You are relaxed and reliable.

You are a family person; for you this is your meaning and purpose in life. Some people might interpret your casual view on the world as lazy, but it isn't. You are reliable and strong willed; you will protect and defend your loved ones and you think time spent relaxing with family and friends is the most important thing. This means you are happy plodding along in a job where you can leave work behind and keep your home life separate, as long as you have enough to be secure. Making people laugh and smile and ensuring everyone is comfortable is what brings you joy.

MAINLY ✳ OWL
You are wise and dependable.

You are studious and love to learn, and find many modern activities frivolous and without meaning. You devour knowledge like an owl eating mice, always hungry for more information and more reasons to study new subjects. You are often relied upon more than others as everyone knows you will get the job done, though at times this frustrates you that no one else is capable or wants to understand how to do these things. You tend to keep to yourself, observing the world like it is an experiment that you are monitoring. With your logical mind, you are prone to over-analyzing each situation and may lack empathy and feeling for others. However, when you do let people in, you are incredibly loyal.

MAINLY ♥ HARE
You are mysterious and unique.

You always feel like the outsider, the world is a place which you find hard to connect with. It's loud, it's bright, there are too many stimulations, and you often want to hide away from it, to escape all of the energy that is vibrating around you. You long for a peace that you aren't even sure exists, but you will keep searching as there is an ache in your heart for something different. Being in large social gatherings with loud people is something you dislike, and you are constantly on the search for like-minded souls to deeply connect with. You are passionate about things that matter to you and although you dislike conflict, you will fight for what is important. People may find you a little odd, your unique style and way of being can make people shy away from you, but you aren't worried by this, as you know you are following a path that is unique for you and you alone.

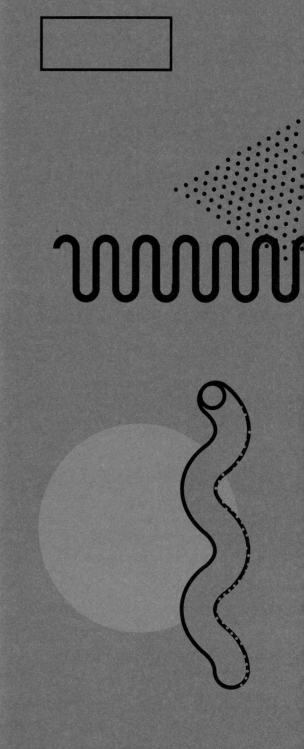

16

WHAT IS YOUR CREATIVE STYLE?

Each of us has a creative style, whether it's cooking a meal, painting a masterpiece, dancing, playing an instrument, or writing a book. We all have something creative in us and all have different ways of showing it. In this fun test you'll identify your creative style and with it, you can try to bring more of it into your life. Creativity in whatever form is what lights us up, and tapping into this energy within us can help us in all aspects of our lives.

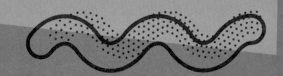

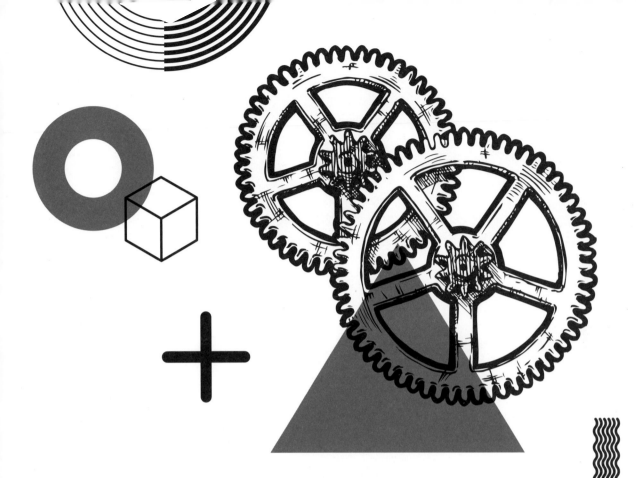

Creativity Types

Creativity is important for all of us. It's what allows us to find solutions to problems, to think of new ideas, and to create a difference in our lives. It's often dismissed as "the arts" that no one really needs, but all roles need creativity.

Being creative is an essential part of being human, but is often overlooked as unimportant, with logic and reasoning being seen to be the preferred routes for careers and education. Yet without creativity, none of our greatest human inventions and ideas would exist. It's essential that everyone finds their creative element, because by doing this it can unleash ideas in other areas. The creative arts fill many people's lives with joy, and these combined with the creative sciences bring us the wonders of the world today. When we look at some of the greatest scientific discoveries, we find that the people behind them, such as Albert Einstein, combined science and art—in Einstein's case, he was a violinist, and this helped him to come up with his theories. Embracing your own creativity is essential to making you feel more fulfilled with your life, although we often put on hold things we love to fit in with societal expectations.

Please go to the resources section (see page 142) to find out more on creativity.

Question 1
Which of the following would you prefer to be?

a. A dancer or actor.
b. An artist or sculptor.
c. A poet or writer.
d. A singer or musician.

Question 2
The most important thing of being creative is...?

a. The desire and need to be creative.
b. To love your work.
c. To connect with who you are.
d. To give others pleasure.

Question 3
If you played a musical instrument, what would you most enjoy about it?

a. Connecting with your inner self.
b. Being able to share your music with others.
c. Being able to get the most out of the instrument.
d. Expressing who you are via the music.

Question 4
When you create something, what do you look forward to the most?

a. Making it come to life.
b. How it makes you feel.
c. Showing your work to the general public.
d. The ideas stage.

Question 5
What would you rather do?

a. Go to the theater.
b. Visit an art exhibition.
c. Join a book group.
d. Attend a musical concert.

Question 6
Which of the following was your favorite subject at school?

a. Languages.
b. Music.
c. English literature.
d. Art.

Question 7
What is your creative outlet?

a. Writing.
b. Singing or playing an instrument.
c. Painting or drawing.
d. Cooking for others.

Question 8
How do you prefer to take in a story?

a. By watching a movie or animation.
b. Reading a book.
c. Listening to an audio book.
d. Reading a graphic novel.

Question 9
What does it take to be creative?

a. Time.
b. Passion.
c. An innate talent, you are born with it.
d. Regular practice.

Question 10
Are you creative?

a. Yes, my career is a creative career.
b. Yes, I do it as a hobby and make time for it after work.
c. Sort of, I dabble in a bit of craft here and there.
d. No, I am not creative at all.

Question 11
Which do you have most of in your home?

a. Art in various formats, such as wall art and ornaments.
b. Books everywhere.
c. Music, e.g. music-playing equipment in every room, or vinyls or CDs, or musical instruments.
d. DVDs, movie-screening equipment, etc.

Question 12
How would people describe you?

a. The singer.
b. The doodler.
c. The entertainer.
d. The dreamer.

RESULTS:

Q1 a✚, b■, c★, d▲	Q4 a■, b▲, c✚, d★	Q7 a★, b▲, c■, d✚	Q10 a■, b✚, c▲, d★
Q2 a■, b▲, c★, d✚	Q5 a✚, b■, c★, d▲	Q8 a✚, b★, c▲, d■	Q11 a■, b★, c▲, d✚
Q3 a★, b✚, c▲, d■	Q6 a✚, b▲, c★, d■	Q9 a★, b✚, c■, d▲	Q12 a▲, b■, c✚, d★

MAINLY ■ ARTIST

A visual dreamer.

The world is a canvas and each day you are lost in its wonder. Everything is about the visual aesthetics around you, what colors go together, how amazing it is that nature knows how to blend its colors. As you go about your day-to-day business, you can see depth in things that others don't, you look with eyes wide open, every aspect inspiring you to paint, to draw, to create. Whatever your chosen medium, you itch to translate the visual world into art that all can see. If you don't currently do anything to release your creativity, then start sketching every day, sign up for an online class or a night class. Take little steps and practice to release a little more of your truth, find the things that make your heart sing.

MAINLY ✚ PERFORMER

A gregarious, theatrical individual.

You love the bright lights, the glitz, and the glamour, you love to give a theatrical display that will take your audience's breath away. You love everything to be vivid and loud. Every time you perform, you want to intoxicate your audience and take them away from their mundane lives to a place of magic and wonder. When not operating in a performing theatrical role, you'll still be known as the one who brings life to the party and to the workplace. But having no outlet can make you frustrated—if you don't do it, consider how you can bring out this side of you in your day-to-day life. Join an amateur dramatics club, do some stand-up comedy. Do something to let your light shine.

MAINLY ▲ MUSICIAN

Quietly confident.

Music is a series of patterns bringing life and magic to sound. You listen to every note in the dawn chorus, you hear magic in the drip of a faucet. The whole world is constantly playing a tune and you always have a song in your head. Whether you play by ear, stick strictly to the sheet music, or sing along to tunes in your home, it is sound and music that have the greatest impact on you. If you don't currently do anything to embrace the musical side of you, then look at what hobbies you can take up. Perhaps some music software on your computer to create your own tunes, learn to play an instrument, or join a choir. Listen for the daily rhythms and patterns in your life to link you to your creativity.

MAINLY ★ WRITER

A quiet soul who shares their dream through words.

Writers love their inner world. You find stories in everything, the way a leaf dances down the road, the change in the wind, or the smile on a stranger's face—all of these can invoke a new character or a new story or a new way to tell your tales. You tend to have a vivid imagination and can happily lose yourself in your world of thoughts and fantasies for hours on end. You can find it difficult to come back to reality and put your ideas on paper, but when you get into the zone, it flows like a river until you are drained and then you need to go back into the inner world to find yourself again.

17

WHAT TYPE OF RULE BREAKER ARE YOU?

Are you the rebel without a cause or are you the person who sticks to the rules? Every one of us has a different relationship with the rules and guidance that exist in our world, and what one person considers a major offence, another will think is perfectly acceptable and they don't know why people are making a fuss. Take this quiz to discover what type of rule breaker you are.

The Four Tendencies

The Four Tendencies was developed by Gretchen Rubin after her investigations into human nature determined that there was one question people should answer to give a deeper understanding of self-knowledge. The question is: "How do I respond to expectations?".

During her research, Gretchen discovered that people tend to fit into one of four tendencies based on their answer to such a question. This tendency defines every area of an individual's life and how they react and behave in a variety of circumstances. Understanding these tendencies allows people to make better decisions, meet deadlines, cope with stress, and interact with others more effectively. More than 2.5 million people have taken her online test, which helps you to determine your tendency. The Four Tendencies are:

Upholders: want to know what should be done
Questioners: want justifications
Obligers: need accountability
Rebels: want freedom to do something their own way

Please go to the resources section (see page 142) to find out more on The Four Tendencies.

Question 1

How likely is it that you wouldn't arrive at an important appointment on time?

a. Very unlikely
b. Fairly unlikely
c. Sometimes
d. Fairly likely
e. Very likely

Question 2

How likely is it that people avoid giving you deadline-based tasks because they know you won't hit the target?

a. Very unlikely
b. Fairly unlikely
c. Sometimes
d. Fairly likely
e. Very likely

Question 3

How likely are you to speak to someone if they are flouting health and safety rules?

a. Very unlikely
b. Fairly unlikely
c. Sometimes
d. Fairly likely
e. Very likely

Question 4

How likely are you to feel frustrated at others for not delivering to their deadlines on projects?

a. Very unlikely
b. Fairly unlikely
c. Sometimes
d. Fairly likely
e. Very likely

Question 5

How likely are you to stick to a timetable or schedule for a vacation?

a. Very unlikely
b. Fairly unlikely
c. Sometimes
d. Fairly likely
e. Very likely

Question 6

How likely are you to adhere to a deadline that has been imposed on you?

a. Very unlikely
b. Fairly unlikely
c. Sometimes
d. Fairly likely
e. Very likely

Question 7

How likely are you to break commitments to others?

a. Very unlikely
b. Fairly unlikely
c. Sometimes
d. Fairly likely
e. Very likely

Question 8

How likely are you to break commitments to yourself?

a. Very unlikely
b. Fairly unlikely
c. Sometimes
d. Fairly likely
e. Very likely

Question 9

In your workplace a dress code is enforced, how likely are you to adhere to it?

a. Very unlikely
b. Fairly unlikely
c. Sometimes
d. Fairly likely
e. Very likely

Question 10

You are asked to adhere to a task—how likely are you to do it exactly as you are supposed to?

a. Very unlikely
b. Fairly unlikely
c. Sometimes
d. Fairly likely
e. Very likely

Question 11

Would you describe yourself as someone who always adheres to the rules?

a. Very unlikely
b. Fairly unlikely
c. Sometimes
d. Fairly likely
e. Very likely

Question 12

When you set a New Year's resolution, how likely are you to keep to it?

a. Very unlikely
b. Fairly unlikely
c. Sometimes
d. Fairly likely
e. Very likely

Q1	a 1, b 2, c 3, d 4, e 5	Q4	a 5, b 4, c 3, d 2, e 1	Q7	a 1, b 2, c 3, d 4, e 5	Q10	a 5, b 4, c 3, d 2, e 1
Q2	a 1, b 2, c 3, d 4, e 5	Q5	a 5, b 4, c 3, d 2, e 1	Q8	a 1, b 2, c 3, d 4, e 5	Q11	a 5, b 4, c 3, d 2, e 1
Q3	a 5, b 4, c 3, d 2, e 1	Q6	a 5, b 4, c 3, d 2, e 1	Q9	a 5, b 4, c 3, d 2, e 1	Q12	a 5, b 4, c 3, d 2, e 1

12-28 GUARDIAN

You believe rules should be adhered to.

Rules are there for a reason, and without them you strongly believe the world would fall apart. When you cook a meal, you adhere to the recipe to the letter and wouldn't consider changing it in any way. You get frustrated with rule breakers and cannot understand why they would flout clear instructions as other people are counting on them, too. If you commit to do something for you or someone else, you will always do it. For you, upholding these rules and instructions gives you a feeling of freedom and the control that you need to feel secure in your life. You don't need others to motivate you, you just do what you need to do. Equally, if you find something in the world with no instructions but it is causing injustice in some way, you will endeavor to get rules in place to stop this. You do find it hard to defer things or delegate them to others and will not flout rules, even when it makes sense to do so.

29-44 ENQUIRER

You view rules individually and question as needed.

You believe certain rules are needed, but some you see more as "guidelines," though it will depend on your own values and beliefs, and what you think is important. You like to get an understanding of why these particular instructions or rules are in place. Then you research why that is, either going into detail with the facts and data, or through conversations to understand if you think this rule should actually apply to you. Anything you do needs to make sense, but once you have understood the logic you will commit to it and deliver with little or no supervision. However, if you decide it doesn't make sense to you, you will develop your own inner instructions and rules that are more appropriate, and you will find ways to justify this. You find it hard to comprehend rule breakers as you want to know why they think the rule shouldn't apply to them, but equally those who uphold the rules frustrate you by not questioning them.

45-60 MUTINEER

You often have a desire to rebel.

Freedom is a key word for you, as your ultimate desire is to go through life having the choice to do what you want, when you want, where you want. It's all about being able to express yourself freely, though it doesn't necessarily mean you are a person who goes around breaking the law. In your dream world you wake up each morning and decide what you want to do, and sometimes you will rebel against yourself and your own commitments to do things for you, even though you know it doesn't make sense. For you it's all about choice, and if you can do stuff in your own way, at your own pace, you will thrive and be a great success, doing unconventional things that make you stand out from the crowd. You like to be different; you like to be unique in your way, even though the person you rebel against the most is yourself.

18

WHAT TYPE OF EMPATH ARE YOU?

Some people seem naturally more attuned to the thoughts and feelings of individuals around them. If someone is going through a crisis, they intuitively know how to respond. Yet for others, this can be very difficult and watching those with more compassion can seem like you are observing a different species. In this test you will discover your empathy level and tips on how you can become more empathic to others.

Empathy

Empathy is the ability to identify, have compassion, and sympathize with other people's, and even animals', situations. It's about understanding the feelings of others. Most people have some level of empathy, but some are more empathetic than others.

Empaths in particular are extremely reactive to the situations around them and have a highly reactive neurological system. In her book *An Empath's Survival Guide*, Judith Orloff talks about how empaths are super responders who absorb not only the positive energies of the world around them, but also the stressful energies. She describes there being three main types of empaths:

- Physical empaths: these people are especially attuned to other people's physical symptoms and can absorb them into their body. They can also become energized by another person's sense of well-being.
- Emotional empaths: these people tend to pick up on other's emotions and can become a sponge for both their positive and negative feelings.
- Intuitive empaths: these people have heightened intuition, telepathy, messages in dreams, and animal and plant communication, as well as contact with the other side.

Please go to the resources section (see page 142) to find out more on empathy and being an empath.

Question 1

Do you find being in large crowds energizing?

a. Never
b. Almost never
c. Sometimes
d. Fairly often
e. Very often

Question 2

Would you say that you overindulge with food or drink in times of stress?

a. Never
b. Almost never
c. Sometimes
d. Fairly often
e. Very often

Question 3

Do you feel you fit in at school/college/work?

a. Never
b. Almost never
c. Sometimes
d. Fairly often
e. Very often

Question 4

When you've been with negative people, do you find you need time away from everyone to recharge?

a. Never
b. Almost never
c. Sometimes
d. Fairly often
e. Very often

Question 5

How often have you been labeled as overly sensitive?

a. Never
b. Almost never
c. Sometimes
d. Fairly often
e. Very often

Question 6

How often do you need to recharge in nature?

a. Never
b. Almost never
c. Sometimes
d. Fairly often
e. Very often

Question 7

Would people describe you as someone who scares easily?

a. Never
b. Almost never
c. Sometimes
d. Fairly often
e. Very often

Question 8

Do you get your energy from being with loud people?

a. Never
b. Almost never
c. Sometimes
d. Fairly often
e. Very often

Question 9

How often do you feel unable to cope with the amount you have to do?

a. Never
b. Almost never
c. Sometimes
d. Fairly often
e. Very often

Question 10

Do you get overwhelmed or anxious?

a. Never
b. Almost never
c. Sometimes
d. Fairly often
e. Very often

Question 11

Do you find that you absorb other people's stress?

a. Never
b. Almost never
c. Sometimes
d. Fairly often
e. Very often

Question 12

Do you react strongly to odors, alcohol, caffeine, medication, and/or chemicals?

a. Never
b. Almost never
c. Sometimes
d. Fairly often
e. Very often

RESULTS:

Q1 a 1, b 2, c 3, d 4, e 5	Q4 a 5, b 4, c 3, d 2, e 1	Q7 a 1, b 2, c 3, d 4, e 5	Q10 a 5, b 4, c 3, d 2, e 1
Q2 a 1, b 2, c 3, d 4, e 5	Q5 a 5, b 4, c 3, d 2, e 1	Q8 a 1, b 2, c 3, d 4, e 5	Q11 a 5, b 4, c 3, d 2, e 1
Q3 a 5, b 4, c 3, d 2, e 1	Q6 a 5, b 4, c 3, d 2, e 1	Q9 a 5, b 4, c 3, d 2, e 1	Q12 a 5, b 4, c 3, d 2, e 1

12-28 APATH
You lack empathy.

You find it very hard to understand other people's emotions and why they are behaving or reacting in the way they do. It feels like they are overreacting to every situation and you can find this frustrating. Everything is about the emotions and you prefer to make all your decisions on facts and logic, but for you it's that inability to understand people which can be problematic. People think you are aloof or uncaring, but that isn't true—you just can't put yourself in their shoes to understand and empathize with what they are going through. You care deeply when it makes sense to do so. You find it hard to express your emotions and this can make it difficult for people to understand your needs and requirements. When you have a particularly low empathic score, find someone you trust who can point you in the right direction. They can explain to you in logical terms the reaction most people have. You may not feel it, but you may be able to understand it.

29-44 BALANCED
You have a balanced view on empathy.

You are able to read emotions in other people and react accordingly. Things such as body language, facial expressions, and the words a person uses will allow you to understand and empathize based on your own experiences. There will be still many occasions when you struggle to have empathy, just because you can't comprehend what the person is going through. However, you can still recognize the main emotions of anger, sadness, fear, hurt, and guilt, as well as happiness, joy, excitement, etc., and because of that you can empathize on the emotion rather than the event. You are generally able to deal with your emotions and those of others as long as they aren't extremes, so for you it's all about understanding why others can have such extremes so that you can comprehend what they are going through.

45-60 EMPATH
You are a highly sensitive person.

As an empath you may find the world too stimulating. Watching the news on TV can be distressing and emotional for you, as you may find that you can feel all of the distress in the world bombarding you. People often criticize you for being "over sensitive" and over the years you may have felt you needed to hide your empathic abilities because of the prejudice against someone like you who is seen as "feeling and caring too much." Being empathetic can feel like both a gift and a curse and it's something you cannot run away from. But when you embrace your natural ability, then you can make it work for you. You may have to say "no" to people and also block negative people or reduce time with these people to protect yourself. As you learn these skills, you can find a new balance in your life.

19

WHAT IS YOUR ROLE IN YOUR FAMILY?

Every family has their own dynamics and every person within a family has a role they play, whether they like it or not. Even as we grow older, leave home, and perhaps have children of our own, we can find we are still adhering to those roles we played in our family during childhood, and don't evolve into our new roles in the family we've created ourselves. In this fun quiz you can determine what role you play in your family to see the impact you have on the people around you.

Family Roles

Family—a place where you hope to feel nurtured and loved, but for many the reality is that family life is a challenge, where you may feel you continue to play a role determined for you in your childhood.

When you consider the archetypical roles that each society has, there are some that traverse the centuries. Mother, father, wife, husband, daughter, son—all conjure an image as soon as you see the word or hear it, based on the society you live in. But our societies have changed, and these roles have evolved, yet our interpretation of them has not. These definitions can be imprinted on us from childhood, coming from our parents, from family history defined before you were even conceived, to societal expectations at our birth. Some of these roles are seen as more acceptable to a man but not to a woman, yet these gender definitions no longer apply in our society. It can be hard to break free of these societal archetypes and until these evolve, our understanding and acceptance of this change can take longer.

Please go to the resources section (see page 142) to find out more on family roles.

Question 1
When people describe you from your childhood, what do they say about you?

a. You made everyone laugh.
b. You were rebellious.
c. You were sensible and worked hard.
d. You were helpful and kind.

Question 2
When life is feeling negative, you cheer yourself up by:

a. Contacting a friend to grumble about life.
b. Focusing on self-care.
c. Pausing and reminding yourself about how lucky you are.
d. Organizing a night out with friends and having a laugh.

Question 3
At a family gathering you are:

a. The entertainment, as someone has to cheer things up.
b. In the corner plotting and gossiping about the family news.
c. In the kitchen helping to serve and clean up.
d. Trying to ensure family rivalries don't ruin the event.

Question 4
What do you think is the most important thing to create a happy family?

a. Knowing what our roles are.
b. A sense of humor.
c. Compassion and kindness.
d. Supporting each other no matter what.

Question 5
A relative is taken ill and needs visiting in hospital—what do you do?

a. Check what they need and take it with you.
b. Arrange to visit and focus on making them laugh.
c. You hate hospitals and try to find an excuse not to go, you'll visit them when they come out.
d. Find out visiting hours and check who is going to ensure not too many visitors at one time, perhaps devising a rota.

Question 6
On a night out with friends you are the one who:

a. Organizes the event.
b. Who will be drunk or lose something.
c. Will be hoping everyone will get on.
d. Chatting to strangers and making new friends.

Question 7
When you have an argument with someone, how do you normally respond?

a. Forget about it and move on.
b. Phone a friend and offload it to them.
c. Try to turn it into a joke and laugh it off.
d. Look at how you can compromise and resolve it.

Question 8
What do you find the most difficult?

a. To not make a joke to lighten the mood.
b. To turn a blind eye when something unfair is happening.
c. To say no to someone.
d. To pretend you are OK when really you are struggling.

Question 9
You admire people who:

a. Who people take notice of and respect.
b. Always seem organized.
c. Who can deal with conflict.
d. Who are happy and content with life.

Question 10
How do you think people might view you?

a. Need to grow up.
b. Too uptight.
c. A people pleaser.
d. As never taking life seriously.

Question 11
A friend tells you about a recent argument they had—how do you respond?

a. Listen and make them feel supported.
b. Change the conversation to something more interesting.
c. Try to make light of it to cheer them up.
d. Give some advice on how to handle it.

Question 12
At school you were:

a. Popular with the teachers.
b. Invited to every party.
c. The shoulder for people to cry on.
d. Always late.

MAINLY ■ STALWART

The one who can be relied upon.

Organized, successful, the sensible one who always gets stuff done. You are the person who organizes the events, the people, and makes sure everyone gets home safely. You are conscientious in everything you do, and it doesn't matter how many plates you are juggling; you will still be the one taking charge of the occasion and ensuring everything runs smoothly. The problem you have is you may struggle to delegate because you don't trust others to do it, but equally you get annoyed at people not asking if you need help. Take a step back and think about who else could take on some responsibility or ask people what they can help with. Stop looking for perfection and try to enjoy the time, not just organize it.

MAINLY ✚ MEDIATOR

You keep the peace.

Everyone comes to you with their problems. You are the wise one who is always there for people, who everyone can rely on in times of need. However, you may find it hard to say no and it's easy to feel overwhelmed with the amount others put on you. This in turn can make you feel resentment which, due to your caring nature, you then feel guilty over. You can be a people pleaser as you try so hard to ensure that conflicts are resolved, even if often you are the one who is continually making the compromises. Try stepping back and getting others to sort out their own dramas—this will stop people coming to you so much, and allow you to focus on your own needs.

MAINLY ▲ UNDERLING

You are considered the baby of the family.

You are the person who is always late but gets away with it because everyone considers you the irresponsible one who hasn't grown up. You carry on through life knowing you have family and friends to bail you out of trouble, which means you take more risks than others to follow your dreams. However, you may find it frustrating that after all this time everyone talks down to you and assumes you are incapable of doing anything more. In particular, family members may be quite patronizing, so when you do undertake more sensible endeavors and achieve things on your own, you find they dismiss it or assume someone helped you. Look at examples of when you have often asked for help from your family and choose one where you'll take control to change their perception of you.

MAINLY ★ JESTER

You are considered the joker in the family.

Every family has a joker within it, and you are that person. Always guaranteed to bring a smile to people's faces, everyone relies on you to lighten the proceedings. Sometimes people think you don't take life seriously enough and you can be frustrated at everyone expecting you to fulfill the happy role. You would like to be taken more seriously and for someone to consider making you smile, as it takes a lot of energy to always be upbeat. But you rarely share your concerns and worries with others and can struggle alone if you are feeling low. Step back sometimes and let others take the center stage so you can have a rest and change people's expectations of you.

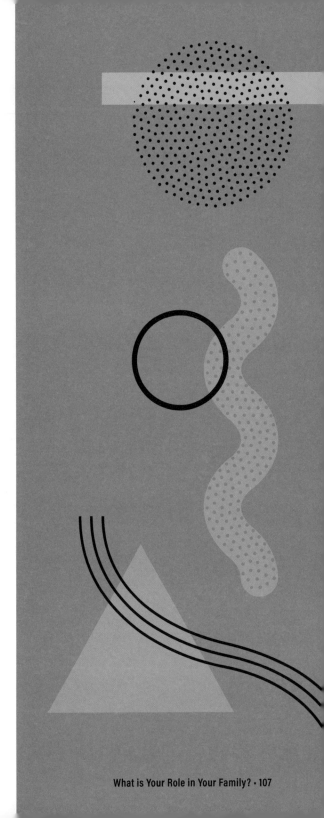

20

WHAT SHOULD I DO WITH MY LIFE?

How often do you here people saying they feel as though they should be doing something different with their lives, something more meaningful? Many people feel they have a life purpose they should be fulfilling. In this fun test you'll get an idea of what your life purpose is so you can consider how you fit that either into your current life or into a new way of living that you carve out for yourself.

The Sparketype™ Assessment

The Sparketype™ assessment was developed by the Good Life Project—an organization that teaches people to lead better lives through community, media, and education—to help people to discover the essential nature of the work they want to do. It's designed to help us to identify the work that lights us up with purpose and drive.

Some people discover this early on in their lives, but many do not and that is where this assessment can help. It's been developed over nearly two decades, drawing from varied fields such as positive psychology, behavioral economics, social science, demography, philosophy, and ancient wisdom traditions, along with thousands of hours of research. When you do the assessment, you're advised what your profile is, which comes in two parts:

Your Primary Sparketype™ is the work that makes you feel fueled by purpose, infused with meaning, fully expressed, and absorbed in a state of transcendent flow.

Your Shadow Sparketype™ is the essential nature of work you may well enjoy and have become highly skilled at, but it's more there to amplify your primary Sparketype™.

The ten Sparketypes™ are:

1. The Maker: driven to create
2. The Scientist: driven to solve
3. The Maven: driven to learn
4. The Essentialist: driven to distill
5. The Performer: driven to perform
6. The Warrior: driven to lead
7. The Sage: driven to teach
8. The Advocate: driven to advocate
9. The Advisor: driven to guide
10. The Nurturer: driven to care

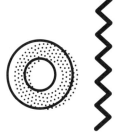

Please go to the resources section (see page 142) to find out more on the Sparketype™ assessment.

Question 1

Your biggest fear when it comes to your career is:

a. Feeling helpless.
b. Being stuck in a boring job.
c. Not being good at your job.
d. Having no control.

Question 2

At school, you enjoyed:

a. Wokring on new things.
b. Being the team captain.
c. Supporting your classmates.
d. Learning new information.

Question 3

Which job did you want when you were at school?

a. Scientist or engineer.
b. Artist, writer, entertainer.
c. CEO, accountant.
d. Doctor, nurse, vet, care-giver.

Question 4

How would your family and friends describe you?

a. Nurturing, caring, helpful.
b. Smart, ambitious, successful.
c. Creative, spontaneous, unique.
d. Intelligent, studious, detailed.

Question 5

If you were creating a garden, what would it be like?

a. You'd develop it over time, and it would be full of color.
b. You'd hire an expert to design something you and your needs.
c. It would be low maintenance and simplistic in design.
d. It would be full of scent and color, a place for friends and family to relax.

Question 6

What do you do to relax on the weekend?

a. You like to have a plan of what you will do.
b. Relax with friends and family.
c. You read non-fiction in your area of interest.
d. Paint, knit, make—anything you can do with your hands.

Question 7

Which of these tasks would make you feel most satisfied?

a. Helping a vulnerable person.
b. Brainstorming new ideas.
c. Leading a team-building exercise.
d. Attending a talk by a specialist in your field.

Question 8

If you went back to school, what would you study?

a. Leadership development.
b. Social care, nursing, teaching.
c. Something creative.
d. Upgraded qualification in your current area of expertise.

Question 9

When you look back on your life, what do you hope to have achieved?

a. That you really made a difference in people's lives.
b. That you were creative.
c. That you continued to learn and grow.
d. That you took the lead and made things happen.

Question 10

What do you find most rewarding about your current role?

a. That you can lead a team.
b. That you really make a difference in people's lives.
c. That you can keeplearning.
d. That it is an amazing outlet for your creativity.

Question 11

If asked about your life lesson, what would your answer be?

a. Look for the beauty in things.
b. Be open and keep learning.
c. Always embrace kindness.
d. Be assertive.

Question 12

If you came into a large amount of money, what would you do with it?

a. Invest in scientific research.
b. Set up your own charity to help the disadvantaged.
c. Set up your own business.
d. Donate to a local gallery or other creative pursuit.

MAINLY ■ EXPERT

You are knowledgeable and inquisitive.

You are the expert in your field, always looking to learn more and to surpass the knowledge of those around you. Whatever your field of expertise, you question, you learn, and you want to know more and embrace and understand the next development. You like to assimilate facts and data and make your own conclusions, theorizing on what the latest advances will include. If anyone needs to know something about your area of expertise, they come to you. If you aren't already embracing this in your current role, look at ways you could become the expert on a topic that you find interesting, and what training you can do to take you to the next level to become the specialist in your organization.

MAINLY ★ NURTURER

You love to help others.

You are caring and supportive, and enjoy supporting and helping those in need. Your true passion in life is tending to the needs of others and this could be in a variety of professions, such as doctor, nurse, care worker, coach, vet, holistic therapist. When you see people growing, healing, and developing, it lights you up inside, and you get a real buzz seeing that the work you do has transformed someone's life. Look at your current role and what you can do to bring more of this nurturing nature into it, perhaps being a mentor or volunteering to help with charity events. Find ways you can embrace the natural nurturer within to light your spark inside.

MAINLY ✚ CREATIVE

You are free-spirited and creative.

You love using your imagination to create something new and unique, and strive to be original in your artistic process. You love to delve into the depth of your creative pursuits and strive for a genuine authenticity in your work, your relationships, and life. You get frustrated with constraints and societal expectations and are constantly looking for ways to break free. If you aren't already using your creativity in your role, look at ways to bring it into your current job or find time for hobbies and interests outside of work to allow you to express yourself.

MAINLY ▲ CONTROLLER

You love to lead.

You're a natural leader and approach life that way. People describe you as being decisive, confident, and assertive. You know what you want, and you will get it. You take charge in all aspects of your life, whether in work where you'll be climbing the leadership ladder to new heights, or at home ensuring your family and friends have someone to rely on to get things done. Whether in a charitable organization or a commercial organization, you will ensure things happen and you will drive everyone to come along on the journey to success with you. In your current role look for ways to take the lead, volunteer to lead a project, or lead a team, continually searching for ways to build on your leadership skills.

21

How do you express your love to your friends, family, and partner? How do you like to receive love? We assume everyone likes to give and receive signs of affection in the same way, but we don't. In this playful quiz you'll discover what your preferences are for giving and receiving signs of affection. Don't just read about yourself, read the other love languages too, so you can understand others and appreciate how they might prefer to receive affection from you.

The Five Love Languages®

The Five Love Languages® was developed by Gary Chapman in his book of the same name, published in 1992. In it he describes how we can all improve our relationships by understanding our emotional communication preferences.

Each of us loves differently and we give and receive love in different ways. It is easy for misunderstandings to occur if we don't understand each other's preference and this is where we can find strain developing in any relationship. There five Love Languages are:

1. Words of affirmation
2. Acts of service
3. Receiving gifts
4. Quality time
5. Physical touch

By singling out your love language, you can understand what it means for you and how you can get more fulfilled connection and intimacy with a loved one. Understanding an individual's preferences can help people to overcome conflict, improve communications, and allow them to become closer, whether this is friendship or with a partner or family member.

Please go to the resources section (see page 142) to find out more on The Five Love Languages®.

Question 1
What makes you feel content?

a. Cuddles with your loved one.
b. When the person you love tells you they miss you.
c. When the person you love helps you out with a task.
d. Getting a surprise gift from a loved one.
e. You and your loved one spending hours alone together.

Question 2
You show love to loved ones by:

a. Focusing on them when alone together.
b. Giving them a special gift.
c. Speaking approvingly about them to others.
d. Lots of physical affection.
e. Planning fun activities together.

Question 3
A loved one hurts your feelings by:

a. Forgetting to get you a thoughtful gift for a key anniversary.
b. Not helping you when you need it.
c. Thinking about something else when you are together, rather than focusing on your time together.
d. Criticizing you.
e. Not giving you a cuddle when you meet after being apart.

Question 4
You feel most loved when a loved one:

a. Helps you with your to-do list.
b. Tells you how important they are to you.
c. Takes the time to truly listen and understand you.
d. Puts their arms around you.
e. Buys you a special gift.

Question 5
When you are feeling low or stressed, you feel better when a loved one:

a. Spends quality moments with you.
b. Gives you a hug.
c. Sends you funny pictures.
d. Does something useful to make your life easier.
e. Says encouraging things to you.

Question 6
How do you feel connected with someone?

a. When they hold hands with you.
b. When you do an activity together.
c. When they do something to accommodate your routine.
d. When they gift you something that is really thought through.
e. When they say something meaningful like "you are mine."

Question 7
Which of the following feels more meaningful for you?

a. Being near someone you love even if doing different things.
b. A loved one buying you your favorite food.
c. A text saying that your loved one loves you.
d. A loved one showing physical affection in public.
e. A loved one doing the chores for no reason.

Question 8

When do you feel appreciated by a loved one?

a. They do something for you, even if it's not something they enjoy.
b. When they give you a genuine compliment.
c. When they dedicate time to you.
d. When they give you a nice massage.
e. When they offer to buy you lunch.

Question 9

What do you look for in a potential partner?

a. Someone who has a good job and is successful.
b. Someone who is flexible with their work so can spend time with you.
c. Someone who can make great conversation.
d. Someone who is kind and caring.
e. Someone who wants to be close to you.

Question 10

What do you love most about your partner or loved one?

a. Their voice.
b. Their hands.
c. Their ambition.
d. Their heart.
e. Their time.

Question 11

Your best friend is moving to a new house—how would you help them?

a. Help them pack and move.
b. Phone them to chat and give moral support.
c. Buy them a beautiful house-warming present of something they really want.
d. Arrange to be there on their first night in their new home so they aren't alone.
e. Spend the evening before the move with them, watching a movie and reminiscing on the good times you had in this place.

Question 12

At the end of a busy day, what would you like your loved one to do for you?

a. Listen to you talk about your day and tell you how much they appreciate you.
b. Give you a massage.
c. Have supper ready.
d. Have bought you flowers.
e. Ordered takeout food and have your favorite movie ready for you to watch so you can be together.

RESULTS:

Q1 a ▲, b ■, c ★, d ✚, e ✳
Q2 a ★, b ✚, c ■, d ▲, e ✳
Q3 a ✚, b ★, c ✳, d ■, e ▲
Q4 a ★, b ■, c ✳, d ▲, e ✚

Q5 a ✳, b ▲, c ✚, d ★, e ■
Q6 a ▲, b ✳, c ★, d ✚, e ■
Q7 a ✳, b ✚, c ■, d ▲, e ★
Q8 a ★, b ■, c ✳, d ▲, e ✚

Q9 a ✚, b ✳, c ■, d ★, e ▲
Q10 a ■, b ▲, c ✚, d ★, e ✳
Q11 a ★, b ■, c ✚, d ✳, e ▲
Q12 a ■, b ▲, c ★, d ✚, e ✳

MAINLY ■ WORDS
Words of encouragement.

You like to receive praise and encouragement in the forms of words and positive messages from your loved ones. This is also your way of showing love, by cheering people on, by chatting with them and telling them how much they mean to you and how much you appreciate them. Listening and hearing their needs, and knowing they are listening and hearing your needs, makes you acknowledge that you are a right match in a loving relationship, whether this is a long-term relationship or a close friendship. However, you can take any negative criticism straight to heart, so you need to be mindful about how you react in these situations.

MAINLY ✚ GIFTS
Receiving and giving gifts.

You adore being showered with gifts, from something as simple as being bought your favorite chocolate to being taken out for a lavish meal. You like it when someone shows their love to you in this way, but equally you love giving people gifts, whether it's sending a bunch of flowers for no reason other than to say that you are thinking of someone. You will find some people don't appreciate these lavish displays and see it as showing off, but for you it's a genuine act of kindness so you can demonstrate you care. Try judging people's reactions as some people might feel uncomfortable with such displays; if that's the case perhaps next time you can do something smaller with a personal note. Their love language may be different to yours, so adapt yours accordingly.

MAINLY ▲ TOUCH
Physical contact.

For you it's the simple acts of physical contact that make you light up. Cuddles and hugs, holding hands, a light touch of your cheek—all of these show you the person who cares for you truly does love you, whether as romantic or friendship love. Equally you love to reach out and hold people when they need you and you can find it difficult to restrain yourself when you see someone in distress, as your default is to comfort them by holding a hand or hugging them close. If you're unsure of another person's love language, ask them if they like to be hugged or prefer a different way of being comforted, so that you can respect their boundaries and understand your own.

MAINLY ★ KINDNESS
Acts of service and kindness.

When someone does something for you without asking, your heart swells, and you look for such kindness toward others in a partner or friend. For you the most attractive feature of another person is their ability to be selfless and kind to others without being asked, and this can make you fall head over heels for someone. You love to help others too, and doing something for someone to relieve their daily burden fills your heart with joy. Some people may mistake this kindness for being a busybody, so ensure you judge another's preferences before jumping in and doing things without asking.

MAINLY ✳ TIME
Spending quality time with loved ones.

Someone who will dedicate their time to you is a gem in your eyes. You don't necessarily have to be doing the same thing together, though you do like this, but just being in the same space, knowing each other is there makes you feel truly loved. When you give out love you do it in a similar way, giving your time to those around you to be with them, even if this is sitting in silence or chatting over a mug of coffee. You love the little things in life and spending time with loved ones is important to you. Ensure you judge other people's preferences too and don't outstay your welcome by imposing your time on others when they don't want it.

22

WHAT IS YOUR PERSONALITY SUN SIGN?

We all know our astrological sign and many of us read our horoscopes to determine what will happen in our lives. Some of us will read them and feel they are a true reflection of who we are. Others will read them and feel that it isn't like you at all and this makes you disregard astrology. In this quiz you will discover your astrological personality based on your preferences, rather than on when you were born.

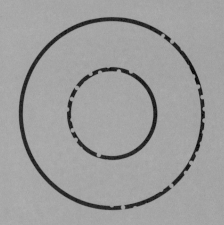

Astrology Personalities

Astrology has been around since the time of the Babylonians, circa 700 BCE, and the first use of the zodiac wheel as we know it today comes from these times. This is another example of categorization of people and their personality, but this time by the date, time, and place of their birth.

Over the centuries astrology has fallen in and out of favor but is now becoming more and more accepted by many people in the world. If you were to ask most people they will know their astrological sun sign and many of you will have an understanding of what the personality is of each of those signs. Whether it is the sexy Scorpios, or the level-headed Capricorns or the flirty Geminis, we all have an unconscious assumption of a person's personality based on this. What many don't realize is that their personality is defined as much by the other signs in the chart at their birth as their sun sign, so their moon sign and their ascending sign will both have a big impact on their personality. For example, a Gemini with Capricorn as their moon sign may come across as quite level-headed.

Please go to the resources section (see page 142) to find out more on astrology.

Question 1

What word best describes you?

a. Leader
b. Level-headed
c. Committed
d. Intelligent
e. Practical
f. Strong
g. Passionate
h. Creative
i. Curious
j. Organized
k. Adventurous
l. Different

Question 2

What is your actual star sign?

a. Pisces
b. Aquarius
c. Aries
d. Cancer
e. Libra
f. Capricorn
g. Taurus
h. Leo
i. Scorpio
j. Virgo
k. Sagittarius
l. Gemini

Question 3

How do you prefer to communicate?

a. You are unpredictable, one moment loving and the next destructive.
b. You are warm and welcoming, but remain objective.
c. You are articulate and your words are well thought through, based on facts and data.
d. You are bubbly and supportive.
e. You like passionate and intense conversations.
f. You are understanding and eloquent.
g. You like to talk in depth about topics that interest you.
h. You are a great, powerful communicator.
i. You are a great listener.
j. You talk about multiple things at once because you have so many ideas.
k. Your words are few, but well thought through.
l. You say it as it is, you are a straight talker.

Question 4

What is your leadership style?

a. Eccentric and unique
b. Steady and reliable
c. Curious and influential
d. Caring and nurturing
e. Bold strategist
f. Organized and determined
g. Harmonious and diplomatic
h. Ambitious and commanding
i. Charming and outspoken
j. Patient, disciplined, and ambitious
k. Intellectual maverick
l. Well-being, wisdom, and wonder

Question 5

What is your dream job?

a. Human rights lawyer
b. Musician
c. Scientist
d. Lifestyle coach
e. Doctor or nurse
f. Author
g. Career advisor
h. CEO or sports captain
i. Teacher
j. Psychologist
k. Radio DJ
l. Diplomat

Question 6

What is your dream weekend retreat?

a. A well-planned visit to museums and exhibitions.
b. An activity vacation.
c. Relaxing on a tropical beach.
d. A volunteering break in nature.
e. Extreme sports that make you feel alive.
f. A luxury upmarket hotel near your home.
g. Visiting an art exhibition and then a meal in a vibrant European city.
h. A hiking break in the mountains.
i. A luxury theater break to see the latest show, with the best seats in the house.
j. A surprise trip where you can explore a new city.
k. A cozy staycation where you can curl up with a good book with friends and family.
l. Anything as long as you can share it with someone.

Question 7

Would you describe yourself as...?

a. Bold, authoritative, and capable
b. Eccentric, sensitive, and sociable
c. Optimistic, extreme, and bright
d. Problem-solving, open-minded, and imaginative
e. Sweet-natured, calm with a steely resolve
f. Ambitious, passionate, and intelligent
g. Idealistic, resolute, and stubborn
h. Inquisitive, competitive, and changeable
i. Hot-headed, energetic, and wise
j. Secretive, forgiving, and honest
k. Generous, indecisive, and argumentative
l. Organized, proper, and living life to the full

Question 8

What's your favorite weather?

a. Thick fog in the night
b. Humid and warm
c. Snow
d. Hot, dry heat
e. Windy days
f. Thunderstorms
g. Sunshine and showers, not too hot and not too cold
h. Fresh spring rain
i. Bright sunshine and clear skies
j. Clear and crisp with frost
k. Icy hail
l. Cloudy skies and mist

Question 9

What is your favorite food?

a. Cheese
b. Hot dog
c. Tacos
d. Spicy potato chips
e. Spaghetti
f. Oysters
g. Dumplings
h. Ramen noodles
i. Burger
j. Mac and cheese
k. Chicken wings
l. Pizza

Question 10

Which is your favorite month of the year?

a. January
b. February
c. March
d. April
e. May
f. June
g. July
h. August
i. September
j. October
k. November
l. December

Question 11

What's your favorite color?

a. Deep red
b. Orange
c. Pastels and pale colors
d. Navy, indigo, and gray
e. Blue, white, and turquoise
f. Vivid blue
g. Pale lilac, lavender mauve, pale yellow, and pale peach
h. Pink and white
i. Deep dark shades of purple, bottle green, maroon, red
j. Green
k. Yellow and gold
l. Black, electric blue, violet, iridescent colors

Question 12

What is your favorite form of exercise?

a. Swimming
b. Captaining a team sport
c. Training for a group charity ride, walk, or run
d. HITT classes
e. Running
f. Barre and/or strength training
g. Core exercises
h. Zumba or dance classes
i. Yoga
j. Pilates
k. Outdoor boot camp
l. Something competitive

RESULTS: WHAT IS YOUR PERSONALITY SUN SIGN?

Q1 a✿,b♣,c★,d✳,e♠,f♥,g╬,h▲,i✛,j✳,k♠,l■

Q2 a▲,b■,c✿,d✳,e♠,f✿,g★,h♥,i✛,j✳,k♠,l✛

Q3 a▲,b■,c✿,d♣,e✛,f♠,g✳,h♥,i✳,j✛,k★,l✿

Q4 a✿,b★,c✛,d✳,e♥,f✳,g♠,h✛,i♠,j✿,k■,l♥

Q5 a■,b✛,c♣,d✿,e✳,f★,g♥,h✳,i✳,j▲,k✛,l♠

Q6 a✿,b✿,c▲,d✳,e✛,f★,g♠,h♠,i♥,j✛,k✳,l■

Q7 a♥,b■,c♣,d▲,e✳,f✿,g★,h✛,i✿,j✛,k♠,l✳

Q8 a✛,b✳,c✿,d✿,e✛,f♣,g♠,h✳,i♥,j✳,k■,l▲

Q9 a✳,b✿,c✳,d♥,e♠,f✛,g♠,h✛,i▲,j■,k✿,l★

Q10 a✿,b■,c▲,d✿,e★,f✛,g✳,h♥,i✳,j♠,k✛,l✿

Q11 a✿,b♥,c✳,d✿,e✳,f♠,g▲,h✳,i✛,j✛,k♠,l■

Q12 a▲,b✿,c■,d♣,e✛,f♠,g✳,h♥,i✳,j✛,k★,l✿

MAINLY ■ AQUARIUS
You are unique.

You are sometimes called quirky, and you love being an individual with your own view on the world. However, this doesn't mean you are a loner, far from it—you are a team player who people gravitate toward due to your thought-provoking conversational topics and your sense of humor. You are passionate about making progress and tackling injustice in the world. When you are on a mission, you get the job done.

MAINLY ▲ PISCES
You are emotional and imaginative.

There is a part of you that is always trying to escape reality, but another part of you that gets swept up in everything going on around you. You are mysterious and intense, with emotions and sensitivities to match. You need to spend time alone or find a place of spiritual tranquility to re-center yourself in times of stress. You like to help people in need and have great compassion. Tap into your creativity through writing, poetry, music, movies, and dance.

MAINLY ★ TAURUS
You are dependable and trustworthy.

You want to be comfortable and make the people around you comfortable, too. You are a hard worker, but when you relax you do it in style and luxury, surrounding yourself with beautiful things, fine foods and drink. Sometimes stubborn, you are also very loyal and dependable but can get stuck in your comfort zone and not want to try anything new. Remember it's good to take some risks, so make them small ones that feel comfortable to you.

MAINLY ✛ GEMINI
You are curious and lively.

You are witty and quick to adapt to any new situation. You are constantly curious and find it hard to focus on one thing at a time. Just like your interests, your emotions and moods can change rapidly and for those who don't know you, these sudden mood swings can come as a shock. Journal about your emotions and your ideas to get all of the information that is racing around out of your head and onto paper.

MAINLY ✳ CANCER
You are emotional and sensitive.

You are the person everyone turns to when they need support and advice. As the nurturer, you know what each person needs—whether it's a hug, a cup of coffee and a cake, advice, or someone to listen, you can adapt and change to support those around you. Sometimes you can be a bit clingy so watch out for this in relationships with others, especially in times of stress.

MAINLY ♥ LEO
You are strong and egotistical.

You want to be first in everything and one of your worst fears is being unimportant. However, people can misinterpret you and don't realize you have a huge heart and are incredibly generous. You need lots of praise and appreciation, which can make people think you are self-centered, but it's just the way you are and how you like to receive love and gratitude. Remember that sometimes it's good to be humble and let others take center stage.

MAINLY ✳ VIRGO
You are graceful, organized, and kind.

You are always analyzing everything, forming opinions and judgments. On the outside, you seem sweet and innocent, but your quick mind never misses a detail. You struggle to ask for help and to receive it due to your perfectionist streak but relax a little—perfection isn't needed all the time. Learn to relax more by spending time in nature or setting yourself fun projects where you can be imperfect.

MAINLY ♠ LIBRA
You are balanced and practical.

You have a balanced view on life but can't stand anything that's unfair, which makes you stand up to injustice in the world. You like to take life at your own pace, which can frustrate others and means you can get embroiled in long debates, losing track of time. This means you can forget to deal with your everyday responsibilities. By becoming a little more organized, it will give you more time to do the things you love.

MAINLY ✚ SCORPIO
You are passionate and independent.

You are energetic and principled and are known for hating people who aren't genuine. You can pick up on the energies of other people, allowing you to read them like a book, seeing every nuance and detail, which can feel a little intimidating to many. Once people do get to know you, they find you are incredibly loyal. Try opening up a little to let people in and build relationships.

MAINLY ♣ SAGITTARIUS
You are strong-willed and adventurous.

You are a free spirit who is open-minded, optimistic, and ambitious. You adore new adventure and look for excitement in the many projects, hobbies, and friends you have. With so many things going on you rarely complete a project, so take some time to finish at least one so that you keep to your promises and commitments.

MAINLY ❖ CAPRICORN
You are hardworking and practical.

You are a very very committed and dependable person, sometimes described as an "old soul" who plays by the rules and follows tradition. It's OK to have fun even if you didn't have to work hard for those small wins, so take a break and share your down-to-earth sense of humor and relax with friends. But also remember to allow them to support you when you are going through tough times, too.

MAINLY ✿ ARIES
If you can imagine it, it can be done.

You are a natural-born leader and inspire all of those around you with your power and confidence, but can be a little bossy and impatient when things don't go your way. You have a loyal set of friends who love to follow you on your latest quest or adventure. Perhaps allow them to take the lead sometimes—it may seem strange at first, but could give you new ideas on how to succeed in future ventures.

23

WHAT IS YOUR CORE ARCHETYPE?

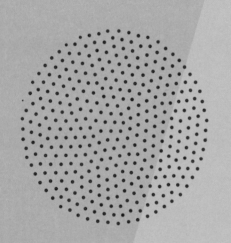

According to Jung's theories of human personality, there are twelve archetypes that define all of humanity. Many of the modern personality type tests we do today are defined from Jung's work. In this quiz you will find out which is the lead archetype that defines your character, and by reviewing your other scores you will see which of the other archetypes are impacting your personality.

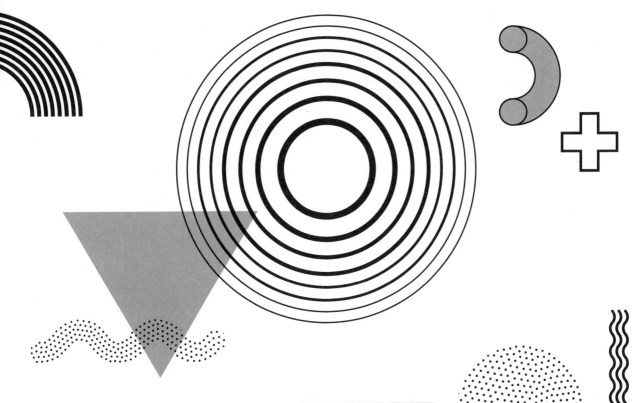

The 12 Core Archetypes

The psychologist Carl Gustav Jung used the concept of archetype in his theory of the human psyche. He believed that universal mythical character archetypes exist within the collective unconscious of people all over the world. Archetypes represent fundamental human ideas of our experience as we evolved; thus, they induce deep emotions.

Jung defined twelve primary types that symbolize basic human motivations. Each type has its own set of values, meanings, and personality traits. The twelve types are divided into three sets of four, namely Ego, Soul, and Self. The types in each set share a common driving source, for example types within the Ego set are driven to fulfill ego-defined agendas.

Most people have several archetypes engaging in their personality construct; however, one archetype tends to dominate the personality in general. It can be helpful to know which archetypes are dominant within ourselves and others, especially loved ones, friends, and coworkers, in order to gain personal insight into behaviors and motivations. The twelve archetypes are:

The Ego Types: The Innocent, The Everyman, The Hero, The Caregiver
The Soul Types: The Explorer, The Rebel, The Lover, The Creator
The Self Types: The Jester, The Sage, The Magician, The Ruler

Please go to the resources section (see page 142) to find out more on Jungian Archetypes.

Question 1
If you were a character in a story, who would you be?

a. The fairy or elf
b. The king or queen
c. The wise one
d. The adventurer
e. The knight
f. The artist
g. The joker
h. The maverick
i. The carpenter
j. The witch
k. The siren
l. The magician

Question 2
What is your favorite creature?

a. Lion
b. Cat
c. Peacock
d. Monkey
e. Dove
f. Swan
g. Owl
h. Raven
i. Dolphin
j. Dog
k. Wolf
l. Magpie

Question 3
What type of books do you like to read?

a. Romantic fiction
b. Children's books
c. Biographies of politicians and other leaders
d. Biographies of sports stars
e. Non-fiction books on new scientific theories
f. Books on art
g. Anti-establishment topics
h. Popular fiction
i. Travel writing
j. Funny stories
k. Historical books on inventions
l. Cookery books

Question 4
What job would you like to do?

a. Fire or police officer
b. Politician
c. Comedian
d. Holistic therapist
e. Nurse or care worker
f. Writer
g. Artist
h. Activist
i. Run a community café
j. University professor
k. Research scientist
l. Travel writer

Question 5
What is something you love to do?

a. Protect your loved ones
b. Do the impossible
c. Confront injustice
d. Be part of a community
e. Make people laugh
f. Go on a romantic date
g. Sing and dance
h. Learn something new
i. Go on adventures
j. Take care of others
k. Lead the pack
l. Make something that has value

Question 6
What is your biggest weakness?

a. Perfectionism
b. Being bossy
c. Being a people pleaser
d. Being a misfit
e. Being too romantic
f. Overthinking
g. Too trusting
h. Being immature
i. Not speaking up
j. Getting too angry
k. Being manipulative
l. Being arrogant

What are the things you care most about?

a. The freedom to make discoveries
b. The ability to explore
c. Knowledge
d. Intimacy
e. Belief
f. Friendship
g. Empathy
h. Power
i. Freedom from oppression
j. Empowering people
k. Expression
l. Laughter and smiles

Question 8

How would your friends describe you?

a. Responsible
b. Creative
c. Adventurous
d. Compassionate
e. Optimistic
f. Wise
g. Passionate
h. Funny
i. Authentic
j. A free spirit
k. A problem-solver
l. Courageous

Question 9

What type of day off do you prefer?

a. Spending time with friends
b. Spending time with family
c. Spending time with your partner
d. Learning a new language
e. Learning a new skill
f. Reading a fantasy fiction book
g. Doing something adventurous
h. Getting involved with a protest that you are passionate about
i. Experimenting with a new idea
j. Doing a charity event
k. Being productive
l. Creating something new

Question 10

What's your greatest fear?

a. Looking weak
b. Being powerless
c. Being left out
d. Living a boring life
e. Not being loved
f. Getting in trouble
g. Looking stupid
h. Being trapped by society
i. Being a selfish person
j. Disorder
k. Being mediocre
l. Accidentally causing trouble

Question 11

What's important to you?

a. Feeling loved
b. Collaborating with others
c. Making the world smile
d. Ensuring others have what they need
e. Making beauty from chaos
f. Leading by example
g. Finding the truth
h. Feeling spiritually connected
i. Leaving your mark on the world
j. Embracing freedom
k. Dreaming
l. Inspiring others

Question 12

How do you like to get things done?

a. By being strong
b. By envisioning a plan
c. By shaking things up
d. By working hard
e. By lightening the mood
f. By engaging people
g. By doing the right thing
h. By researching and creating a process
i. By trying things out
j. By helping others
k. By taking control
l. By using your skills

RESULTS: WHAT IS YOUR CORE ARCHETYPE?

Q1 a■,b✿,c★,d▲,e✛,f✧,g♣,h✚,i♠,j✳,k♥,l✻
Q2 a✿,b✚,c✛,d♣,e■,f♥,g★,h✳,i✳,j♠,k▲,l✧
Q3 a♥,b■,c✿,d✛,e✧,f✧,g✚,h♠,i▲,j♣,k✳,l✳
Q4 a✛,b✿,c♣,d■,e✳,f♥,g✧,h✳,i✳,j★,k✳,l▲
Q5 a✛,b✳,c✚,d♣,e♣,f♥,g■,h★,i▲,j✳,k✿,l✧
Q6 a✧,b✿,c✳,d▲,e♥,f★,g■,h♣,i♠,j✛,k✳,l✛
Q7 a✳,b▲,c★,d♥,e■,f♠,g✳,h✿,i✛,j✛,k✧,l♣
Q8 a✿,b✧,c▲,d✳,e■,f★,g♥,h♣,i♠,j✛,k✳,l✛
Q9 a♣,b♠,c♥,d▲,e✧,f■,g✛,h✚,i✳,j✳,k✿,l✧
Q10 a✛,b✚,c♣,d♣,e♥,f■,g★,h▲,i✳,j✿,k✧,l✳
Q11 a♥,b♠,c♣,d✳,e✧,f✿,g★,h■,i✛,j▲,k✳,l✛
Q12 a✛,b✳,c✚,d♣,e♣,f♥,g■,h✳,i▲,j✳,k✿,l✧

MAINLY ■ THE INNOCENT
Free to be you and me.

Like a young child, you are bright, open-minded, happy, and full of positivity. A real ray of sunshine, you light up a room and make everyone feel welcome. You are considered kind, trusting, and humble, though you fear punishment and need validation. You can be too trusting and a little naive as you look for the good in everything.

MAINLY ★ THE SAGE
The truth will set you free.

You are always questioning and seeking the truth by using your inquisitive mind to sift through the facts and data. Always wanting to understand more, you are constantly on a quest for knowledge via books, taking classes, or debating ideas. You fear being misled or being ignorant on a topic and because your wisdom and intelligence are your shining force, as long as you don't become yourself paralyzed by inaction, you can make real change in your world.

MAINLY ▲ THE EXPLORER
Don't fence you in.

You are an independent go-getter who doesn't conform to traditional ideas, preferring to live your life in your own way, on your own terms. You have a strong desire to improve the world with your exploratory discoveries and fear being penned in and locked down to a mundane life. This can make you something of a misfit or an outcast. You inspire a sense of wonder in others with your authenticity, independence, and ambition.

MAINLY ✛ THE REBEL
Rules are made to be broken.

You aren't afraid to be different and if you see a change that needs making in the world, you'll fight for it, however uncomfortable that might be. You want to change things that seem wrong in favor of something with more promise. But remember that what is a "freedom fighter" to one is a "terrorist" to another.

MAINLY ✳ THE MAGICIAN
You make things happen.

You're a dreamer who has the ability to turn your ideas into realities. Your charisma and unique point of view allow you to do the impossible and you create your own magic in order to better understand the universe you live in. Sometimes playing about with the unknown can cause a disaster, making you seek to manipulate things in order to fulfill your vision. You always have the skills to create a win-win situation.

MAINLY ✚ THE HERO
Where there's a will, there's a way.

Your strength, bravery, boldness, and discipline mean you often become a champion of those weaker than yourself. You are always looking to prove yourself and you hate being weak, vulnerable, or cowardly. Sometimes you can seem to overcompensate for any shortcomings by becoming dictatorial or seeking out a fight. But in your heart, you will prove your worth through brave acts of courage that improve the world.

MAINLY ♥ THE LOVER

You're the only one.

You delight in intimacy, sensuality, and emotion, whether that is through elevating simple moments, like a walk in the backyard, into delightful experiences. You fear being alone because that would suggest you are unwanted and unloved, and because of this you can lose yourself in relationships or become a bit of a people pleaser. You have a real sense of commitment to all of your relationships.

MAINLY ♣ THE JESTER

You only live once.

You love to brighten people's days using your humor to conquer the hearts and minds of others. Your main aim is to liven up the world by spreading joy, though it can sometimes mask your own hidden sadness. You can fear that you will bore people with the normality of your life, which can lead to you wasting your life on frivolity rather than genuine connection.

MAINLY ♠ THE EVERYMAN

All men and women are created equal.

You are happy to support and collaborate with others because of your belief that all people should have equal rights and opportunities. You are honest, authentic, and hardworking and have a lot of empathy for other people. You have a deep need to belong which can leave you feeling anxious.

Sometimes you'd prefer to lose your individuality in order to fit in, making you cynical about others' distinctiveness.

MAINLY ✳ THE CAREGIVER

Love your neighbors as yourself.

You act as a mentor or guide to others, supporting and defending those around you. You are always the person who is the shoulder to cry on and you protect and care for anyone within your friendship circle. Consistent, trustworthy, and responsive, you constantly want to be of service to others, but this can lead to people taking advantage of your good nature. Your compassion makes everyone love you.

MAINLY ♣ THE RULER

Power isn't everything, it's the only thing.

You aren't afraid to take control and you understand how people and power function together. A natural leader, you are politically savvy and well connected, you know how to create prosperity by exerting control, but in the right way. You fear chaos and if you think your subordinates may be about to challenge you, you can become quite overbearing. But under normal circumstances you lead responsibly and use your skills to improve the world.

MAINLY ❖ THE CREATOR

If you can imagine it, it can be done.

You are intensely creative and quite persuasive, and you can be found in many different creative roles, such as writer, designer, musician, or architect. You are always on the lookout for solutions to the world's disorder, but sometimes your perfectionism and fear of coming up with a poor idea can paralyze you. At your best you combine your creativity, imagination, and inventiveness into a harmonious combination.

24

WHAT IS YOUR PERFECT WORKOUT?

Have you ever wondered why some people can run and find it enjoyable, while others find it a chore? Or why some like to do a high intensity workout in a large group, whilst others prefer to work out on their own? In this quiz you can find out your workout personality and discover the exercise that best suits you, helping you to find a way to keep fit that links with your personal preferences.

Workout Personality Type

Your personal preferences will determine what exercise you find enjoyable and what you don't, yet devising a workout for your personality is rarely taken into consideration. Now more research is being done to understand the psychology of exercise so everyone can find what they enjoy.

When bombarded with images from the media, we can feel like we should be partaking in the latest exercise trend, but in a world geared to people with a preference for extroversion and for schedules and logic, we can easily forget that for many people exercise needs to be something different. For some the loud music in a gym is incredibly offputting as their sensitive nature finds this draining, not stimulating. A scheduled workout can make the rebels out there metaphorically run a mile. Some people want exercise for their body, but many want it for more than that, to help with their mind and also their soul. As more and more research is conducted, the link between mind, body, and soul is gaining widespread acceptance and with it the need to find exercise that meets your personal needs, not the latest trend.

Please go to the resources section (see page 142) to find out more on exercise and personality.

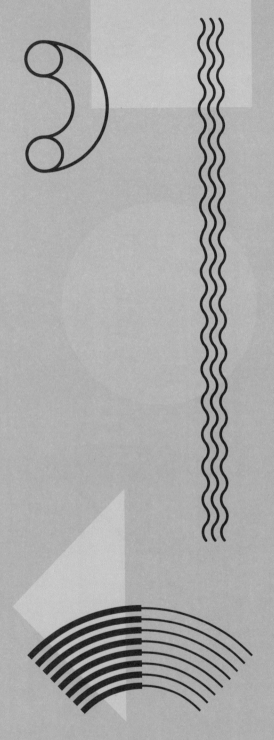

Question 1
What is your motivation for exercising?

a. Improve my mind and body connection.
b. Destress and reconnect.
c. Reach goals and build strength.
d. Make friends and have fun.
e. For the adrenaline rush.

Question 2
What is in your gym bag?

a. Walking boots.
b. Yoga mat.
c. Fitness tracker.
d. Change of clothes.
e. Various gear for different pursuits.

Question 3
Who do you like to work out with?

a. With your teammates.
b. With your personal trainer.
c. On your own.
d. With your best friend or partner.
e. In nature.

Question 4
What is a perfect evening for you?

a. Going out for drinks, then to a club or live music event.
b. Going to the gym and an exercise class.
c. A meal with friends.
d. Alone, reading a book.
e. Summer evenings, having a BBQ with loved ones.

Question 5
What is your ideal workout?

a. Something that makes you sweat.
b. Something that calms your mind.
c. Something that grounds you.
d. Something fun.
e. Something that's not boring.

What do you look forward to on the weekend?

a. Meeting up with friends and family.
b. Spending time in nature.
c. Heading out on an adventure.
d. Quiet time to paint, read, or do mindfulness.
e. Taking part in a competition.

Question 7
What are your mornings like?

a. Chaotic, dashing around trying to remember everything you need for the day.
b. Up bright and early to get to work, so you can finish early for your next excursion.
c. Quiet and peaceful—you like to ease into the day.
d. A highly organized routine to fit everything in.
e. You always start by opening the windows to let in the fresh air.

Question 8
What is your reason for missing a workout?

a. Only injury would stop you.
b. Out of the season for your sport or too much socializing.
c. Too much stimulation and not finding anywhere peaceful.
d. Bad weather (and it has to be really bad).
e. Being distracted with something more interesting.

Question 9
What is your mental approach to exercise?

a. It brings you inner peace.
b. If you're with friends, they motivate you to do it.
c. Beating your previous targets.
d. You get excited at trying new things.
e. It makes you feel alive.

Question 10
What music do you like to listen to when working out?

a. Fast pumping music to get your rhythm moving faster.
b. The sound of your own heartbeat as the adrenalin rush kicks in.
c. Bird song.
d. Shouts from your teammates.
e. Nothing but your own breathing.

Question 11
Which of these quotes inspires you the most?

a. "The mountains are calling, and I must go." John Muir
b. "The strength of the team is each individual member. The strength of each member is the team." Phil Jackson
c. "If you can't win, make the guy ahead of you break the record." Evan Esar
d. "In solitude I find my answers." Kristen Butler
e. "Real freedom lies in wilderness, not in civilization." Charles Lindbergh

Question 12
What do you eat after working out?

a. Protein shake or bar.
b. A healthy salad.
c. A treat with friends.
d. Food cooked on a camp fire.
e. Soup and snacks.

Q1	a★, b■, c▲, d✱, e✚	Q5	a▲, b★, c■, d✱, e✚	Q9	a★, b✱, c▲, d✚, e■
Q2	a■, b★, c▲, d✱, e✚	Q6	a✱, b■, c✚, d★, e▲	Q10	a▲, b✚, c■, d✱, e★
Q3	a✱, b▲, c★, d✚, e■	Q7	a✱, b✚, c★, d▲, e■	Q11	a✚, b✱, c▲, d★, e■
Q4	a✚, b▲, c✱, d★, e■	Q8	a▲, b✱, c★, d■, e✚	Q12	a▲, b★, c✱, d■, e✚

MAINLY ■ NATURE
You love fresh air in your lungs.

Exercising outdoors is what is most important to you, whether this is on your own or with loved ones. You find the fresh air and wind stimulate your mind, body, and soul, bringing calm and destressing you from your day-to-day worries. You're happy to be out in all weathers, which adds to the appeal of working out in nature. You relish seeing the change in the seasons and modify the tempo of your workouts depending on what is happening in the environment around you. Whether you are going for a walk, running, wild swimming, or playing soccer on the beach, the great outdoors stimulates you to look after your health and well-being.

MAINLY ✚ ADVENTURE
You are an adrenalin junkie.

For you, exercise is all about getting your next adrenalin high. You may do day-to-day stuff in the gym to keep you going but you crave the weekends and vacations to get out there on your next adventure. This could be mountain climbing, surfing, or extreme mountain biking, but all of it gets your heart pumping and you're constantly looking for the next thrill. You may prefer doing this on your own or with a close friend or loved one who also loves the thrill, but however you do it, you like the excitement and the challenge that gives you this natural high.

MAINLY ▲ COMPETITOR
It's about hitting goals.

For you exercise is all about hitting your goals. You have a set plan and goals and targets you want to achieve, whether that's losing weight, gaining muscle, or beating your latest time. You thrive on competition and like taking part in events and love a challenge. You are always looking for ways to better yourself and improve, which is why you may like working out with others or one to one with a personal trainer. Once you hit one target, you then start aiming for the next, whether it's running a 5k or a marathon, you will train to get yourself to a place to be the best you can.

MAINLY ✳ SOCIAL
Exercise is about having fun.

When it comes to exercising, it's all about the social experience, and breaking a sweat while having fun with others is more important than the workout itself. Whether it's in a Zumba or yoga class, doing spin, or being part of a soccer team, you enjoy the camaraderie of group activities and the social side that comes with it. You have a bit of a competitive streak and love being part of a group of people aiming for the same goals. Without this you'd find exercise difficult, and feeling like you would be letting other people down is what motivates you to keep going.

MAINLY ★ SOLITUDE
Exercise is for quiet reflection.

You like to spend time alone, to clear your mind, to destress, and to reconnect your mind, body, and spirit. You find loud music and lots of chatter offputting, so you tend to avoid gyms which you find over-stimulating. For you it is about feeling every movement in your body and being in the moment with your breath. When you have to exercise in a world where others are present, you may block the world out with your own music or audio books to keep within your inner world. Whether you are doing yoga, Pilates, swimming, walking, or running, exercise is a form of meditation for you that helps you bring balance to your life.

25

Do you know someone who is particularly narcissistic? Perhaps you sometimes wonder if some of the things you do put you on the narcissism scale? It can be a difficult balancing act to determine when to have admiration and love for yourself and when it becomes an obsession. We're told to love ourselves more, but not too much or you'll be labeled as an egotistical narcissist. This quiz allows you to discover where you are on the narcissism scale so you can get the balance right for you.

Narcissism

Narcissism is described as the excessive interest in or admiration of yourself and your physical appearance. In psychological terms this is referred to as Narcissistic Personality Disorder (NPD), which is characterized by a long-standing pattern of grandiosity, a complete lack of empathy.

This disorder can either be in a fantasy world or actual behavior and often comes with an overwhelming need for admiration. People with this disorder often believe they are of primary importance in everyone else's life and to anyone they meet. For a person to be diagnosed with NPD by a specialist, they tend to need to meet five or more of the following symptoms:

- Have an exaggerated sense of self-importance.
- Is preoccupied with fantasies of unlimited success, power, genius, beauty, or ideal love.
- Believe that they are "special" and unique and can only be understood by, or should associate with, other special or high-status people.
- Require excessive admiration.
- Have a very strong sense of entitlement.
- Is exploitative and manipulative of others.
- Lack empathy.
- Is often envious of others.
- Regularly shows arrogant, conceited behaviors or attitudes.

Please go to the resources section (see page 142) to find out more on narcissism.

Question 1

I am an extraordinarily talented person.

a. Strongly agree
b. Agree
c. Neither agree or disagree
d. Disagree
e. Strongly disagree

Question 2

I can make anyone believe anything I want them to.

a. Strongly agree
b. Agree
c. Neither agree or disagree
d. Disagree
e. Strongly disagree

Question 3

There is a lot I can learn from other people.

a. Strongly agree
b. Agree
c. Neither agree or disagree
d. Disagree
e. Strongly disagree

Question 4

It makes me uncomfortable to be the center of attention.

a. Strongly agree
b. Agree
c. Neither agree or disagree
d. Disagree
e. Strongly disagree

Question 5

I find it easy and enjoyable to manipulate people.

a. Strongly agree
b. Agree
c. Neither agree or disagree
d. Disagree
e. Strongly disagree

Question 6

I can talk my way out of anything.

a. Strongly agree
b. Agree
c. Neither agree or disagree
d. Disagree
e. Strongly disagree

Question 7

I like to show off my body.

a. Strongly agree
b. Agree
c. Neither agree or disagree
d. Disagree
e. Strongly disagree

Question 8

I usually get the respect that I deserve.

a. Strongly agree
b. Agree
c. Neither agree or disagree
d. Disagree
e. Strongly disagree

Question 9

I will make others feel bad to make me look good.

a. Strongly agree
b. Agree
c. Neither agree or disagree
d. Disagree
e. Strongly disagree

Question 10

I find compliments embarrassing.

a. Strongly agree
b. Agree
c. Neither agree or disagree
d. Disagree
e. Strongly disagree

Question 11

I like showing off if I get the chance.

a. Strongly agree
b. Agree
c. Neither agree or disagree
d. Disagree
e. Strongly disagree

Question 12

I am always right.

a. Strongly agree
b. Agree
c. Neither agree or disagree
d. Disagree
e. Strongly disagree

RESULTS: HOW SELF-AWARE ARE YOU?

Q1 a 5, b 4, c 3, d 2, e 1	Q4 a 1, b 2, c 3, d 4, e 5	Q7 a 5, b 4, c 3, d 2, e 1	Q10 a 1, b 2, c 3, d 4, e 5
Q2 a 5, b 4, c 3, d 2, e 1	Q5 a 5, b 4, c 3, d 2, e 1	Q8 a 1, b 2, c 3, d 4, e 5	Q11 a 5, b 4, c 3, d 2, e 1
Q3 a 1, b 2, c 3, d 4, e 5	Q6 a 5, b 4, c 3, d 2, e 1	Q9 a 5, b 4, c 3, d 2, e 1	Q12 a 5, b 4, c 3, d 2, e 1

12-23 YOUR NARCISSISM LEVEL IS LOW

You may have low levels of confidence and sometimes lack self-esteem, but you have a deep empathy for people around you. Be careful as you may be a target for narcissists who might want to manipulate your kind nature. Although having a low score in narcissism is not a bad thing, it's worth considering how you can develop yourself to be more assertive and support yourself. If you have negative people around you belittling your efforts, look at how you can spend less time with them and more time with people who support you.

24-36 YOUR NARCISSISM LEVEL IS AVERAGE

You are self-aware and understand how important it is to be assertive and have confidence and self-belief, but also be empathic to others. You have what it takes to be a natural and gentle leader when the situation arises, and sometimes you need to take up this mantel to protect vulnerable people around you. Keep listening, be modest, and be kind, and you will continue to develop into a balanced individual who can be successful without "walking over others."

37-47 YOUR NARCISSISM LEVEL IS QUITE HIGH

You may think that narcissism is an extreme form of self-love—it isn't. Narcissism has nothing to do with self-love. It is to do with you perceiving that there is an extreme lack of resources, such as self-love, so you try to keep them for yourself. It is great to have ambition and it is great to have confidence, but it shouldn't come with a lack of empathy. Look at your answers and chat them through with an honest friend. Are you being a little narcissistic? What is causing you to behave like this? Look at ways you can keep the balance between being a success but without losing your empathy and kindness for people around you.

48-60 YOUR NARCISSISM LEVEL IS HIGH

You are someone who has a high level of self-importance. You know you are destined for greatness and you will achieve it at any cost. You have no issue with manipulating people to do your bidding—your view is that if they are stupid enough to do it, then that is their problem. You love to be the center of attention and you know you deserve it; anyone who doesn't agree is just envious of your achievements. You find it difficult to read other people's emotions but feel this isn't a skill that is important as you strive to world domination. OK—so you've scored highly in this quiz, but be honest, are you proud of your score or did you answer like this to be center stage and get a laugh. If you recognize these traits, see what you can do to be a little kinder and less self-centered each day.

WHAT NEXT?

So, you've done all the tests in this book and you've found out new things about yourself and those around you. But what do you do next?

When you first start looking at personality tests it can feel overwhelming—the information you have been given isn't entirely new to you, but it does remind you of who you are. So the first thing to do is to pause, to reflect on what you have rediscovered about yourself.

Were there any contradictions? Were there any surprises? You need to consider the frame of mind and environment you were in when you took each test as this can impact your answers, and also examine if you were answering how you think you should rather than honestly.

From the tests you completed, go back and review the ones you enjoyed the most. Read through them again and have a look at the resources section to see if there is anything more you can learn and discover about the particular tests that you might find useful to explore in more detail.

Look at the answers for the other personality types on these tests so you can understand others, as this can help you in your communications with family, friends, and coworkers. Perhaps you've already had some light-bulb moments where you now understand why someone you know behaves in the way they do. Remember not to judge or categorize people based on your assumptions, but be self-aware of how you interact with people and try to put yourself in their shoes before reacting.

When you review your answers and when you delve into personality type testing in more detail, you may want to consider what areas you would like to pursue as areas for growth. Perhaps it's self-belief, or reviewing your current career options? The choice is yours. Choose one to be your developmental focus for the next few weeks, then read and reread the information pertaining to this. It takes time to comprehend these things and it is only as we utilize this information on a regular basis that we can make changes in life.

It's worth noting that there are four fundamental stages of learning:

1) Unconsciously unskilled—You don't know what you don't know (where you may have been before reading this book).
2) Consciously unskilled—You know that you don't know (and this is where you might be now).
3) Consciously skilled—When you know how to do something through conscious involvement (i.e. you know more about these development opportunities, but you have to think about it to utilize them).
4) Unconsciously skilled—When you know how to do something, through unconscious habit (when it becomes second nature to you, and you do it without consciously thinking about it—your aim).

Many people read a book, do a personality type test once, and expect instant results regarding how it will impact their life. But if you take into consideration the stages of learning, just like riding a bike or learning to drive, it takes time before it becomes second nature. Knowing this allows you to keep repeating and rereading and learning, until the areas you have identified as opportunities for improvement become part of your expanded range of preferences. Just as if you had to write with your non-preferred hand for a long time, you would eventually be as good at writing with it as with your preferred hand.

There is so much you can do when you understand your personality preferences, from self-development to making changes in your life. Though there is far too much to cover in this small book, there are plenty of resources on the following pages to point you in the right direction, and you can always work directly with a coach to go into this in more detail.

Hopefully this book has explained to you the concepts of personality testing and allowed you to understand it in more detail. It's introduced you to a range of researched testing programs that can be used within your home and working life to point you in the direction of learning that may be useful for you in the future.

This book is here to open your eyes to what is out there; it's a fun way to reconnect with who you are, but also with friends and family. It's the sort of book you can use as an ice breaker for a new group of people or as an activity with friends and family.

Ultimately it's here to give you an insight into what personality type testing is all about. Hopefully it has also opened your eyes to new possibilities and from this you may identify a spark, a new beginning, a fresh opportunity. Embrace it, there is no moment like the present to follow your dreams, your hopes, and your aspirations.

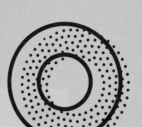

RESOURCES

Books

Introducing Jung: A Graphic Guide by Maggie Hyde, Michael McGuiness, and Oliver Pugh (ICON Books, 2015)

What Would Freud Do? by Sarah Tomley (Octopus Publishing Group, 2017)

Gifts Differing: Understanding Personality Type by Isabel Briggs Myers with Peter B. Myers (Davies Black Publishing under license of CPP Inc, 1995)

The Wisdom of the Enneagram by Don Richard Riso and Russ Hudson (A Bantam Book, 1999)

The Empath's Survival Guide by Judith Orloff MD (Sounds True, Inc, 2017)

Emotional Intelligence by Daniel Goleman (Bloomsbury, 1996)

The Four Tendencies by Gretchen Rubin (Two Roads, 2017)

The Good Psychopath's Guide to Success by Dr. Kevin Dutton and Andy McNab (Bantam Press, 2014)

Online

The Five Factor Personality Model
www.psychologistworld.com/personality/five-factor-model-big-five-personality

www.themojocoach.co.uk
Haulwen Nicholas is a qualified NLP coach, hypnotherapy practitioner, Time Line TherapyTM practitioner, Myers Briggs® Indicator practitioner, and Sacred Money Archetypes® coach.

Myers-Briggs®, MBTI®, Myers-Briggs Type Indicator
www.themyersbriggs.com
www.myersbriggs.org

16 Personalities
www.16personalities.com

Insights® Discovery
www.insights.com

The Enneagram®
www.enneagraminstitute.com

The Process Communication Model®
www.processcommodel.com

Neuro-linguistic Programming (NLP)
www.abh-abnlp.com
www.unleashyourpotential.org.uk

Eysenck Personality Questionnaire (EPQ)
www.hanseysenck.co.uk

The HEXACO Model of Personality Structure Inventory
hexaco.org

The Birkman Method
www.birkman.com

Emotional Intelligence
www.danielgoleman.info/topics/emotional-intelligence

Hogan Personality Inventory, Development Survey, Motives, Values, and Preferences Inventory
www.hoganassessments.com/assessment/motives-values-preferences-inventory

Sacred Money Archetypes®
www.sacredmoneyarchetypes.com

Psychopathy
www.kevindutton.co.uk

Stress
www.stress.org
https://www.nimh.nih.gov/health/publications/stress/index.shtml

Positive Thinking
www.mayoclinic.org/healthy-lifestyle/stress-management/in-depth/positive-thinking/art-20043950

Spirit Animals
www.mindbodygreen.com/articles/how-to-find-your-spirit-animal

Creative Types
www.mycreativetype.com, a quiz by Adobe®

The Four Tendencies
www.gretchenrubin.com

Empathy
www.drjudithorloff.com

Family Roles
https://www.psychologies.co.uk/whats-your-family-role

Sparketype™ Test
www.goodlifeproject.com/sparketest/

The Five Love languages®
www.5lovelanguages.com

Astrology Personalities
www.astrostyle.com/zodiac-signs/

The 12 Core Archetypes
www.soulcraft.co/essays/the_12_common_archetypes.html

Workout Personality
www.webmd.com/fitness-exercise/features/whats-your-workout-personality#1

Narcissism
www.psychcentral.com/disorders/narcissistic-personality-disorder/

Trademarks and Copyright Credits

Myers-Briggs®
MBTI, Myers-Briggs Type Indicator, Myers-Briggs are trademarks or registered trademarks of the MBTI Trust, Inc in the United States and other countries.

Insights® Discovery
Trademark or registered trademark of The Insights® Group Limited.

The Enneagram Institute®
Trademark or registered trademark of The Enneagram Institute®.

The Process Communication Model® (PCM)
Trademark or registered trademark of Atria Group.

The HEXACO Model of Personality Structure Inventory
Copyright © Kibeom Lee, Ph.D. and Michael C. Ashton, Ph.D.

The Birkman Method
Copyright © Birkman International, Inc.

Hogan Personality Inventory, Development Survey, Motives, Values and Preferences Inventory
www.hoganassessments.com/assessment/motives-values-preferences-inventory/

Sacred Money Archetypes®
Trademark or registered trademark of Kendall Summerhawk.

The Four Tendencies
Copyright © Gretchen Rubin.

Sparketype™ Test
Trademark or registered trademark of The Good Life Project.

The Five Love Languages®
Trademark or registered trademark of Northfield Publishing.

INDEX

"LIFE ISN'T ABOUT FINDING YOURSELF. LIFE IS ABOUT CREATING YOURSELF."

George Bernard Shaw